ANATHEMA MARANATHA

✠ ✠ ✠

ANAT✠HEMA

Anathema Maranatha

CHRISTIANITY AND THE IMPRECATORY ARTS

Martin Duffy

Images by Johnny Decker Miller

Three Hands Press
2022

First Three Hands Press edition, October 2022.

Book design by Joseph Uccello and Daniel A. Schulke.
Typesetting by JFU.

ISBN-13: 978-1-945-147-39-5 (softcover)

Printed in the United States of America.

www.threehandspress.com

Contents

I FORM THE LIGHT, AND CREATE DARKNESS: I MAKE PEACE, AND CREATE EVIL: I THE LORD DO ALL THESE THINGS.

Isaiah 45:7

Introduction

WITCHCRAFT IS OFTEN defined as a practice oppositional in nature to society's conventional religious and cultural norms, with its beliefs and rites being inversions of the religion against which it stands. Thus, in the Western world, the witch's rites of cursing are typically considered inversions of Christian prayers and blessings: one coin, two sides. Yet, cursing is not unique to 'witchcraft', for it is an art that has long been practiced by holy men and women of Christian denominations. However, whilst the witch's power to curse was thought to proceed from the Devil and his minions, the holy curse was instead presumed to work by grace of God and the intercession of his holy retinue.

Imprecations of the Christian faithful are frequently encountered in scripture, hagiographies, miracle stories, chronicles, annals, and other narrative sources. This is perhaps unsurprising, as imprecatory rites can be found in most, if not all, religious traditions the world over.

For the purposes of this work, curses are categorised as being one of three types:

Direct curse – Where the curse is addressed directly and explicitly to the victim, for example, "*I curse you.*"

Analogical curse – Where the curse is expressed through spoken or physical analogy, in which a symbolic deed unleashes the imprecatory power. A verbal example of this type would be "*as the fruit rots on the tree, so too may you rot away.*" A physical example would be the burial of a fruit so that it rots away, a gesture which may or may not be accompanied by a corresponding spoken formula.

Prayer curse – Where the curse involves a supplication or command to a higher power, in which the spiritous agency is expected to execute the curse on the individual's behalf, e.g., "*may God strike you down.*" Prayer curses sometimes draw upon scripture for inspiration, and may contain a narrative formula, i.e., an account or litany of the various curses and punitive miracles the god or spirit has previously meted out, such as "*as you plagued the Egyptians with frogs, gnats, flies, diseased cattle, boils, storms of hail and fire, locusts, and darkness—and even as you caused the death of their firstborns—so too may you wreak desolation and misfortune on my enemies.*"

I

The Wrath of God in Scripture and Apocrypha

WHEN LOOKING FOR scriptural antecedents of cursing, professed Christians need look no further than the Bible, a book replete with examples of vengeful maledictions inflicted upon those disobeying God's law. Indeed, even a cursory reading of the Bible demonstrates that God and his prophets were just as ready to curse as to bless, and their maledictions were typically hurled at apostates, heretics, sinners, opponents, traitors, and the deities and representatives of competing faiths.

These biblical curses are effectively the *opposite* of blessings: just as good fortune is bestowed in exchange for conforming to God's will, so too are curses laid upon those opposing him. Herein, benedictions and maledictions are revealed as opposite sides of the one coin—a carrot and stick by which to maintain God's will upon earth.

Whilst an exhaustive list of such curses would be prohibitively long, some of the more colourful examples include:

Cursing the serpent for tempting man, thereby causing him to go forth on his belly and consume dust for the remainder of his days (*Genesis* 3:14).

Cursing Eve for eating the forbidden fruit, causing the pain and sorrow of conception to be multiplied, and making it so she will be dominated by her husband (*Genesis* 3:16).

Cursing the ground after Adam ate the forbidden fruit from the tree, so that man would have to toil to eat (*Genesis* 3:17).

Cursing Cain for killing Abel (*Genesis* 4:11-16).

Pledging to curse those who would curse Abram (*Genesis* 12:3).

Pledging to curse all those who are wicked (*Proverbs* 3:33).

Pledging to curse those who do not give honour to the Lord's name, and to curse their blessings (*Malachi* 2:2).

Cursing Israel for not paying tithes and offerings (*Malachi* 3:6-10).

Pledging to curse those who disobey God's commands. The raft of consequences that will ensue include cursing the sinner's basket and kneading bowl, cursing their offspring (known as a generational curse), blighting the produce of their ground, cursing their cattle and their cattle's offspring, causing everything they do to be unsuccessful until they are destroyed and ruined, bringing disease upon them until they perish, inflicting them with madness and confusion, causing them to be defeated before their enemies, and causing their loved one to be raped (*Deuteronomy* 28:15–68).

This list is chiefly restricted to those examples specifically described as a 'curse'. The word 'curse' is generally used in scripture to translate the Hebrew verbs '*alah*, '*arar*, and '*qalal*, which refer to a variety of acts whereby God or man invoke evil against an individual or group for reasons of a religious, secular, or personal nature. However, in addition to deeds explicitly described as curses are the many punitive events God rained down upon man to punish him for his transgressions, such as the Flood, the destruction of Sodom and Gomorrah through fire and brimstone, the turning of Lot's wife into a pillar of salt, the slaying of Judah's firstborn for being 'wicked in the Lord's sight', and the famine and plagues visited upon Egypt.

Like his Father before him, Jesus was no stranger to cursing. For example, he cursed the cities of Chorazin, Bethsaida, and Capernaum for rejecting him and not repenting (*Matthew* 11:20–24 and *Luke* 10:10–15). He also cursed a fig tree for being barren, which caused it to wither and die, and then proceeded to expound on how this demonstrated the efficacy of prayer (*Mark* 11:11–14, 20–25 and *Matthew* 21:18–22), saying:

> Have faith in God...if anyone says to this mountain, 'Go, throw yourself into the sea,' and does not doubt in their heart but believes that what they say will happen, it will be done for them. Therefore I tell you, whatever you ask for in prayer, believe that you have received it, and it will be yours.

This prayer for magical effect, wherein God is implored to lay a curse on Christ's behalf, is comparable to the way witches allegedly prayed to the Devil to curse their victims. Here, the prayer is used a vehicle to convey desire to the preternatural agency with which one is in a familiar relationship.

In the *Infancy Gospel of Thomas*, a 2nd century biographical gospel detailing events from Jesus' childhood, the son of God is presented as a powerful wonderworker with the capacity for being a malevolent trickster. Within the text, the child Jesus not only demonstrates great knowledge, the power to resurrect the dead, heal wounds, produce a feast from a single grain, and bring inanimate clay objects to life (even as God brought forth man from the clay), but also a callous tendency to curse those who cross him. For example, when he was five years old, Jesus collected water from a stream into ponds, and made the water instantly pure. When the son of a scholar used a willow branch to drain the water from these pools Jesus became angry and said, "from this moment you too will dry up like a tree, and you'll never produce leaves or root or bear fruit." On pronouncement of this analogical curse, the boy instantly withered away into a corpse.

On another occasion a boy accidently bumped into Jesus whilst running through the village, which angered Jesus, causing him to exclaim, "you won't continue on your journey", and thereafter the boy immediately fell down dead. The villagers were understandably worried about having such a powerful and capricious child in their midst and told Joseph he must either teach Jesus to bless and not to curse, or else take his family and leave the village. Joseph had no desire to leave the village, and so rebuked Jesus for killing the villagers' children. However, Jesus was displeased with being scolded and said, "I know these are not your words, and I'll keep quiet for your sake, but these people must take their punishment", and with that all those who had complained to Joseph became instantly blind. Joseph was angered by Jesus' actions and so grabbed his ear hard, but this only further infuriated Jesus, who threateningly exclaimed, "don't you know that I don't really belong to you? Don't make me upset."

Sometime later, a teacher sought to teach Jesus the alphabet. Becoming exasperated by the child's bumptious behaviour, the teacher struck him on the head. Jesus, ever quick to anger, cursed him and the teacher fell down dead. Upset by these events, Joseph decided that Jesus mustn't be let outside, "because those who annoy him end up dead."

In another incident, Jesus' brother, James, was sent by Joseph to gather some firewood, and whilst doing so was bit by a viper. As James lay dying on the ground, Jesus blew on the bite, which caused the pain to stop. The snake then suddenly burst apart and James immediately recovered. A comparable story occurs in *The First Gospel of Infancy*, where a child (who is revealed as Simon the Canaanite) is bitten by a snake whilst gathering firewood and, being close to death, goes to Jesus. Jesus calls the serpent from the woods and commands it to, "go and suck out all the poison which thou hast infused into that boy." Submitting to the request, the serpent crept to the boy and took back all its poison. However, despite this act of compliance, Jesus still cursed the serpent and caused it to immediately burst asunder and die.

The characterisation of the child Jesus as a severe and somewhat capricious individual is also found in folklore and folksong. Illustrative is the English folk ballad, *The Bitter Withy* (Roud 452), which Cecil Sharp collected from John Hands and his family in the Snowshill area in 1909. It has also been collected from numerous sources around the West Midlands and from various gypsy communities. The events of this apocryphal carol ultimately derive from the *Infancy Gospels* and tell how three rich young lords refused to play ball with the child Jesus because:

> We are all lords' and ladies' sons,
> Born in a bower and hall,

And you are nothing but a poor maid's child,
Born in an ox's stall.

With a tear in his eye, Jesus replies, "I'll make you believe in your latter end, as I am an angel above you all." Then, using the beams of the sun, Jesus builds a bridge across the river and runs over it, the event found in the early 7th century *Gospel of Pseudo-Matthew* and also in a 13th Century poem known as the *Vita Rhytmica*.

The three young Lords attempt to follow Jesus across the bridge, but fall into the water and drown. When the boys' mothers tell Mary what Jesus has done, she puts him across her knee and gives him three thrashes with a bunch of withy (willow) twigs. Jesus then curses the willow, saying:

O bitter withy, O bitter withy,
That causes me to smart.
O the withy shall be the very first tree,
To perish at the heart.

This latter verse constitutes an origin story for willow's propensity to rot from the inside out, and is comparable to other religious narratives explaining peculiar arboreal characteristics. Amongst such etiologies is the belief that poplars shake easily because they didn't tremble at the crucifixion (or in other versions because the crucifix was made of poplar wood), and that elders were cursed to be crooked and weak because Jesus' crucifix was made of its wood (or alternatively because Judas hanged himself from an elder).

This carol wherein Jesus commits multiple infanticides was popular with rural English folk for many years. Some believe this was a result of the snobbish lords getting their comeuppance at the hands of a poor underdog, i.e., they took comfort in the idea that God was on the side of the poor and humble, and not the lords and ladies. In similitude to the *Infancy Gospel*, this carol portrays the child Jesus using preternatural means to punish or kill those who offend him, which some have charitably interpreted as a portrayal of Jesus' struggle to come to terms with his unique condition—a human born with a divine nature. Others perceive the carol as a parable concerning power and the necessity of learning to wield it wisely.

The ability to invoke formidable maledictions was also credited to God's chosen representatives, and reference to the prophets' dual power to confer restorative blessings and deleterious curses is found in *Numbers*. When Balak, the King of Moab, hired a prophet named Balaam to help deal with the mass of Israelites about to enter his land, he said to the prophet:

> Now come and put a curse on these people, because they are too powerful for me. Perhaps then I will be able to defeat them and drive them out of my land. *For I know that whoever you bless is blessed, and whoever you curse is cursed* [emphasis mine]. (*Numbers* 22:6)

Unsure what to do, Balaam spoke to God, and asked his advice. God told Balaam not to place a curse on the Israelites because they are blessed, and in accordance with God's wishes the prophet duly refused to lay the curse, despite Balak's pleas and promises of financial reward. God then told Balaam to go before Balak and speak only the words He put into his mouth, words which were a prophecy of blessing upon the Israelites. Notably, in this narrative the malediction is not foiled by the prophet's inability to lay a curse, but rather his choice to obey God's commands. Similarly, when Paul cursed the Jewish high priest Ananias, saying, "God shall smite thee, thou whited wall." (*Acts* 23:3),[1] he quickly repented, not because he had no right to curse, but rather because the Old Covenant prohibited the cursing of the Israelites' ruler (*Exodus* 22:28).

Other scriptural examples of curses laid by God's representatives include the curse Noah placed upon his grandson, Canaan, as punishment for his father's transgressions (*Genesis* 9:25). Another is the curse Joshua

1 A whited wall was one that had been dusted with lime dust, which during the 1st Century was done to eliminate odours from walls that were set-aside for the public to urinate against. The walls of sepulchres were also whited to reduce the odour of the dead, and reference to this is found in *Matthew* 23:27, where Christ compares the hypocritical Scribes and Pharisees to whited sepulchres. Paul's words may thus have been intended either as an insult (by likening him to a wall against which people urinated) or to insinuate he was a hypocrite (by recalling Christ's use of the word).

pronounced on those who would undertake to rebuild Jericho, vowing that he who laid its foundations would lose his first-born son, whilst he who set up its gates would lose his youngest (*Joshua* 6:26). According to *Revelations*, even in death the spirits of the prophets and saints called out to God for vengeance on those who had slain them:

> And when He broke the fifth seal, I saw underneath the altar the souls of those who had been slain because of the word of God, and because of the testimony which they had maintained; and they cried out with a loud voice, saying, "How long, O Lord, holy and true, wilt Thou refrain from judging and avenging our blood on those who dwell on the earth?" (*Revelation* 6:9–10)

A demonstration of the apostles' power to curse is also found in *Acts* 5:1–11. It tells how Ananias and his wife Sapphira secretly withheld some of the profits made from selling their land, even though all monies were supposed to be put in a common pot for donation to the needy (*Acts* 4:32). When Peter confronted Ananias about why he had lied to the Holy Spirit and chosen to withhold the money, Ananias immediately fell down dead at Peter's feet. Three hours later Sapphira arrived home unaware of what had happened, and when Peter asked her how much the land was sold for, she also lied, and in consequence fell down dead. Whilst this narrative lacks the pronouncement of a specific curse, the immediacy of the deaths after Peter's confrontation strongly implies a correlation of 'cause and effect': for example, Peter's harsh words had sufficient power to constitute an unspoken curse. This interpretation is supported by scripture, which reports the incident caused a great fear of the Lord to sweep the church. Of all examples of apostolic cursing, this is perhaps one of the harshest, for Peter confronted Sapphira knowing his previous confrontation had resulted in Ananias's death.

Also found in *Acts* (8:9–25) is an incident concerning Simon Magus, who practiced sorcery in Samaria during the 1st Century CE. Due to Simon's amazing feats people heeded his words, and declared him 'the divine power called the Great Power'. However, after witnessing the powers and miracles of Philip the Evangelist, Simon and the people of Samaria were quickly converted to Christianity. Upon news of this mass conversion, Peter and Paul visited Samaria to instill its people with the Holy Spirit. When Simon saw how the Spirit was given to supplicants through the laying on of hands, he desired to have the same ability, and offered the apostles money in exchange for this power. Peter was angered by this, and thundered:

> May your silver perish with you, because you thought you could buy the gift of God with money!

Some scholars have noted a similarity between Peter's response and those curses exacted through the analogical formula of sorcery, wherein what happens to one thing is caused or persuaded to happen to another, for example: 'just as this happens to X, so too may it happen to Y', which in this case manifests as, 'just as your silver perishes, so may you perish also'.

With this curse ringing in his ears, Simon repents and asks Peter to pray to the Lord on his behalf so the things Peter said would not happen to him, and the curse would be lifted. Herein is found an example of a curse being nullified by a blessing from the one who pronounced it.

Several apocryphal works also detail this confrontation between Simon the Magus and Peter, but don't end quite so favourably. In the *Acts of Peter*, Simon is presented as a powerful sorcerer with the ability to levitate and fly, and whilst he is performing this feat the apostle Peter prays to God to stop his flying. As a result of Peter's 'curse-prayer' Simon immediately falls to earth, breaks his legs in three parts, and eventually dies. A comparable tale is recounted in the *Acts of Peter and Paul*, although in this variant Simon's fatal fall causes him to be 'divided into four parts.'

The canonical book of *Acts* contains a more direct apostolic curse, which is pronounced during a confrontation between Paul, who had been sent on a mission by the Holy Spirit, and Bar-Jesus ('son of Jesus'), a Jewish sorcerer, imposter, and false prophet. During the confrontation, Paul looked Bar-Jesus in the eye and said:

> O child of the devil and enemy of all righteousness! You are full of all kinds of deceit and trickery. Will you never stop perverting the straight ways of the Lord? Now look,

> the hand of the Lord is against you, and for a time you will be blind and unable to see the light of the sun.

At that moment, a mist and darkness came over Bar-Jesus, and he groped about, seeking someone to lead him by the hand (*Acts* 13:4–120).

Akin to other direct curses, Paul's curse is made in public and is an emphatic enunciation of the curse to be laid, 'now look...you *will* be blind and unable to see the light of the sun', a pronouncement which is immediately fulfilled. As a result of this punitive miracle, the proconsul who witnessed it was convinced of the Lord and His power.

Like many scriptural examples, this curse is not fulfilled by Paul but by 'the hand of the Lord'—an otherworldly power—which is reminiscent of the way witches were supposed to lay their curses by power of the Devil. The act of invoking a deity or other spiritous agency to strike down an adversary is a common component of ancient magic, and often takes the form of a prayer for justice, wherein the spirit or deity is adjured to punish a wrongdoer, right a perceived wrong, or avenge injustice. By evoking a numinous agency to mete out this 'divine justice' it also serves to transfers the responsibility of the curse and its repercussions to the evoked entity.

Some have suggested this trio of apostolic curses from *Acts* were intended to be read in continuity with one another, conceivably to illustrate the early church's attitude towards transgressive behaviour, particularly as all three have an element of deceit and greed.

Modern Christians have often sought to interpret such imprecatory speeches as prophecies rather than direct curses. By downgrading the apostle's role in the unfolding drama from curser to prophet (from causative agent to prognosticator), they work to diminish the apostle's direct responsibility for the grim outcomes of their pronouncements. However, whilst the apostles' imprecatory speeches are devoid of any specific binding formulae, they clearly constitute dramatic words of power capable of securing immediate and miraculous, albeit punitive, effect. Moreover, the apostles' maledictions are portrayed as having sufficient import to inspire fear, conversion, and belief, which suggests that in antiquity (at least) God's chosen representatives were considered to have authority to pronounce and facilitate curses, even as they conferred benedictions. Yet, despite the prophets' capacity and authority to use words of power to deliver blessing and imprecation, their deeds were only legitimised when carried out in accordance with God's will.[2]

One of the more explicit biblical curses is that recounted in *2 Kings* (2:23–24), and concerns God's prophet Elisha. Whilst walking along a road, Elisha was confronted by a group of youths from a nearby town, who jeered at the prophet, saying, "Get out of here, baldy!" Angered, Elisha turned back to look at the youths, and called down a curse upon them in God's name. Immediately, two bears came from the woods and ripped forty-two of the youths limb from limb.

Many Christians have sought to distinguish biblical maledictions from 'pagan' curses by arguing the latter were made in vengeance against personal slights, whilst the former were made for the greater good, in other words, to overcome the obstacles standing in the way of spreading the Word and establishing God's kingdom on earth. However, it is somewhat difficult to explain how children poking fun at a prophet with a bit of name-calling constitutes a serious obstacle to the Christian faith, let alone how causing forty-two of the adolescents to be mauled to death by bears is a reasonable or measured response to this slight.

Another clear malediction is found in *1 Kings* (17:1), wherein Elijah proclaims "as the Lord, the God of Israel, lives, whom I serve, there will be neither dew nor rain in the next few years except at my word." This pronouncement of divine judgement was made in revenge for Israel's rebellion against God, and demonstrates an ability to control the weather for the purposes of making the land barren and inhospitable.

Kings also contains an exemplar of a malediction affecting the victim's physium. There are several such examples in the Bible, which in similitude to folk curses cause withering of limbs, lameness, and blindness. In *1 Kings* 13:4, when King Jeroboam reached out to seize the prophet who decried the idolatrous altar in Bethel, his arm withered and dried up so that he could not move it. This punitive miracle is evocative of God's threat in *Zechariah* 11:17, "Woe to the worthless shepherd, who deserts the flock! May the sword strike his arm and his right eye! Let his arm be completely withered, his right eye utterly blinded!"

2 Benedict H. M. Kent, 'Curses in Acts; Hearing the Apostles' Words of Judgement Alongside 'Magical' Spell Texts'.

A more aggressive malediction is that pronounced by the prophet Jeremiah, who appeals to God for divine retribution against those who had wronged him, imploring his Lord to 'pull them out like sheep for the slaughter, and set them aside for the day of slaughter' (*Jeremiah* 12:3). *Jeremiah* (19:1–11) also contains an incident resembling an analogical curse. It combines the spoken word with a powerful symbolic act and is reminiscent of the execration rites carried out by ancient peoples. God commands Jeremiah to buy a potter's earthenware jar, and to smash it before an audience of elders and senior priests. He was then to tell the audience that God was going to bring calamity upon them, and would break the people and their city, "even as one breaks a potter's vessel, which cannot again be repaired." Whilst the scripture renders this episode as a prophecy, the people would have been familiar with contemporaneous execration rites wherein vessels, bowls, and figurines were smashed, and it is likely such practices would be at the forefront of their mind when hearing of Jeremiah's actions. Moreover, the pronouncement of God's word, and the symbolic act of smashing the jar, clearly served to set in motion the calamitous events expressed by word and deed.

Another malediction is found in *1 Corinthians* (16:22), when at the summation of a letter, Paul the Apostle declares:

> If anyone does not love the Lord Jesus Christ, let him be Anathema. Maranatha!

The word 'anathema' is rendered in numerous translations as 'accursed', and signifies the individual shall be cast out of the church and accursed by Christ on Judgement day, only to suffer eternal damnation. *Maranatha* is an Aramaic word, which can be translated as either 'Our Lord has come', 'Our Lord is coming', or 'Our Lord, Come!' Whilst some translate the passage as, 'let him be accursed in the coming of the Lord', or read it as a warning that one should listen to Paul's words because the Lord is coming. Others believe *Maranatha* to instead be an appeal to the Lord to 'come forth'—an evocation. Interestingly, based on the teachings of the 4th Century monk St. John Cassian, the British priest John Main recommended a form of Christian meditation wherein one silently and repeatedly recited the prayer-word *Maranatha*, meaning

'Come Lord', as a mantra in the form of *Ma-ra-na-tha*. This effectively served as an evocation of Christ within the body. Some consider the use of the un-translated foreign word *Maranatha* to be commensurate to the Graeco-Roman use of *voces mysticae* in curse tablets and magical incantations.

Particularly common in the Bible are imprecatory prayers intended to secure the destruction of those deemed sinful and wicked. For example, Moses prayed, "Rise up O Lord! And let Thine enemies be scattered, and let those who hate Thee flee before Thee." (*Numbers* 10:35). More severe is the imprecatory prayer the prophet Jeremiah made against his opponents (*Jeremiah* 18:21–23):

> ...give their children over to famine, and deliver them up to the power of the sword; and let their wives become childless and widowed. Let their men also be smitten to death, their young men struck down by the sword in battle. May an outcry be heard from their houses, when Thou suddenly bringest raiders upon them; for they have dug a pit to capture me and hidden snares for my feet. Yet Thou, O Lord, knowest all their deadly designs against me; do not forgive their iniquity or blot out their sin from Thy sight. But may they be overthrown before Thee; deal with them in the time of Thine anger!

Of all biblical maledictions, most challenging to rationalise are the generational curses, the punishment of offspring for their parents' transgressions. A particularly heavy curse is that of Original Sin, the ancestral curse that stems from Adam and Eve's transgressions in Eden. Passages asseverating generational curses are found throughout the Bible. For example, in *Exodus* 20:5, God says, 'I, the Lord your God, am a jealous God, punishing the children for the sin of the parents to the third and fourth generation of those who hate me', which sentiment is also expressed in *Deuteronomy* 5:9. Moreover, in *Exodus* 34:7 and *Numbers* 14:18, it is proclaimed, 'Yet he [God] does not leave the guilty unpunished; he punishes the children and their children for the sin of the parents to the third and fourth generation.'

Belief in generational curses endured long after biblical times, and make frequent appearances in British folklore. Such tales are seldom found in relation to poor families, but typically concern wealthy families descended from wicked aristocratic ancestors, and detail the fall of their accursed house into wrack and ruin. Some of these accounts end with the family line dying out, whilst others conclude with an ill-fated descendant seeking to escape their inherited curse through piety, prayer, sacrifice, and devout faith, an endeavour which usually met with success. Such accounts thus serve as moralistic tales, which not only affirm God's wrath towards the unfaithful, but also the forgiveness He proffers those yielding to His word.

Particularly rich in maledictions are the Apocrypha, wherein God's prophets are portrayed wielding miraculous powers akin to those of Christ. Illustrative is an example from the apocryphal *Acts of John* 37–47 (2nd Century), wherein John the Apostle enters the Temple of Artemis at Ephesus on a festival day. Whilst the celebrants were dressed in white, John wore black, which impiety offended the temple attendants, causing them to make an attempt on his life. Escaping their clutches, John took to a pedestal and addressed the baying and bloodthirsty crowd, declaring:

> Ye all say that we have a goddess...pray then to her that I alone may die; but if you are not able to do this, I will call upon my own god, and for your unbelief, I will cause every one of you to die.

Terrified, the temple attendants pleaded for their lives, so John implored God to show them mercy, "for they have been made to err." Immediately the altar of Artemis split asunder, and her sacred vessels fell to earth, causing them to be smashed to pieces, along with the idols of Artemis and seven other gods. Half the temple then fell down, which crushed the priest of Artemis. This great display of power caused the celebrants to declare:

> We know that the God of John is the only one, and henceforth we worship him, since we have obtained mercy from him.

After these events, John remained in Ephesus to instruct the new converts in the Christian faith. He also raised the priest of Artemis from the dead, which inspired him to convert to Christianity and become one of John's disciples.

Another example from the Apocrypha is related in the *Acts of Thomas* (early 3rd century). Whilst attending a wedding, the apostle Thomas was struck by a cup-bearer. The affronted apostle looked upon the cup-bearer and said, "My God will forgive you for this wrong in the world to come, but in this world He will show His wonders, and I will soon see the hand that struck me dragged along by dogs" (*Acts of Thomas* 6). The cup-bearer then repaired to a well to draw water, but whilst there he chanced upon a lion, which slew him and tore the limbs from his body. A number of dogs seized the dismembered limbs, and a black dog picked up the cup-bearer's severed right hand, which he carried back to the wedding banquet—where the apostle was feasting—for all to see (*Acts of Thomas* 8).

The plenitude of maledictions preserved in scripture demonstrates the act of cursing is not sinful in itself, but rather becomes 'sinful' when there is discord between the curse's motivation and God's law. This is to say, whilst it is fundamentally licit to call down God's wrath to avenge and punish transgressions—those things the Christian faith considers 'wrong' or 'sinful'—it is illicit to wish evil on others without proper justification. Yet, even the scriptures contain several curses that challenge this principle, including the curse evoked by the prophet Elisha, which God answered by sending forth two bears to tear apart the forty-two children who called his prophet 'baldy' (*2 Kings* 2:23–24).

2

Execrations in the Lives of Saints, Priests, and Monks

The magico-religious arts of cursing are practiced by peoples of most religious persuasions, and typically involve the petitioning of the familial deity or deities in order to visit vengeance upon one's opponent(s), whose deity or deities are rendered as evil and devilish opposers. In the West, this dualistic antagonism is manifest in the battle between God and the Devil, the principles of light and darkness, who command the celestial forces of heaven and the chthonic forces of hell.

In pitting the people of one faith against another, god(s) are set against god(s), and the outcome of these mortal battles, which are wagered by the preternatural weaponry of imprecatory prayer and ritualistic malediction, serve to establish whose god(s) are more powerful. This is to say, when a curse is pronounced in a god's name and proves successful, it affirms the deity's superior power, and that of its priests and followers. This affirmation of power serves to bolster the reputation of the god amongst its people, emboldening them to rally behind their tutelary spirit and its priesthood. Beyond encouraging conversion and quelling the thoughts of those contemplating allegiance with other gods, these successes also foster a reputation of indomitability, which has the potential to stave off future opposition.

In Western theological terms, this narrative is rendered as a battle between God and the Devil, and incidents wherein 'righteous' prophets possessed by the Holy Spirit confront Devil-possessed wrongdoers effectively serve as microcosmic correlatives of this conflict between the two oppositional powers. In relating tales concerning the triumph of

God's ordained representatives over devilish peoples by power of holy malediction, the Bible promotes the idea of God's supremacy, and demonstrates His power over those who do the Devil's work. This narrative is also woven throughout the Christian hagiographies, which record the legends accreting about various saints, some of whom are Christianised versions of earlier 'pagan' gods or spirits.

The tales of the hagiographies typically take their inspiration from biblical episodes and seek to promote the saint's many God-given powers. Whilst rich in tales illustrating the saints' magical power to heal, these panegyrical biographies are also replete with accounts of the curses they doled out to wrongdoers, which attests to the saints' dual power to bless and curse. As Gregory of Tours wrote of St. Martin, 'his power is shown in the punishment of the foolish just as in the grace of healing.'

Whilst church authorities have often sought to differentiate ecclesiastical maledictions from lay-curses, it is notable that the curses of saints are typically motivated by the same kind of wrongdoing that incited the imprecations of common folk, such as theft, deceit, insult, and murder. Moreover, the saints' curses frequently occasion the same punishments as those exacted by magic and witchcraft, including blindness, paralysis, sterility, insanity, withering of limbs, and death.

Particularly rich in punitive miracles are the hagiographies of the Welsh and Irish saints, with an especially great number being associated with Ireland's most famous saint, St. Patrick. For example, in the 9th Century work, *The Tripartite Life of St Patrick*, it is recounted how the saint 'fasted against' a cruel slave owner named Trian who refused to amend his ways. The saint then cast his spittle upon a rock, which caused it to break into three parts, and said:

> Two thirds of the fasting on the rock, a third on the king and on his fort and on his district. There will be of Trian's children neither king nor crown-prince. He himself [Trian] shall perish early and shall go down into bitter hell.

Herein, St. Patrick essentially commanded the deleterious effects of his fast to be sublimated and redirected towards Trian in the form of a curse. Shortly after St. Patrick's fast, Trian was riding his chariot when his horses dragged him off into Loch Trena, where he drowned.

It is said Trian remains trapped there until the vespers of Doomsday, at which time he will be condemned to eternal damnation.

The practice of fasting against an enemy is also found in a number of witchcraft cases. It was used to secure the death of a specified victim, and was known as 'the black fast' or St. Trinian's Fast.[1] For example, in 1519 Elizabeth Robinson of Bowland threatened to carry out a black fast against Edmund Parker. Also, in 1538, Mabel Brigge of East Riding (Yorkshire) carried out a black fast against Henry VIII and the Duke of Norfolk. Mabel admitted she had on another occasion undertaken a fast against a man, and he had broken his neck before her fast was over.

Fasting also features in the life of the Welsh saint, David, who once made camp with his men on land claimed by Prince Boya. Angered by their presence, Prince Boya's wife sent several of her female servants to seduce the saint and his monks by bathing naked before them. St. David fasted against these women in order to repel them, and in one account it is written the women thereafter 'walked with the wind upon the path of death', which is to say they were cursed.

Another of St. Patrick's curses is recorded in the Middle Irish work, *De Ingantaib Érenn* ('On the Wonders of Ireland'). Whilst preaching Christianity in the Irish kingdom of Ossory, one clan opposed St. Patrick more than any other, and when he preached the faith they would howl at him like wolves. St. Patrick retaliated by praying to God to punish the clan. God acquiesced, and cursed the wrongdoers by temporarily turning them into wolves, during which period of time they lived and ate like beasts but with the wit and wiles of man. Accounts of the werewolves of Ossory are preserved in a number of other early Irish, English, and Norse works.

Another Irish saint with a predilection for cursing was St. Mochuda, who hurled a great number of maledictions in his lifetime. For example, in the later life of Colmán Ela, it is recounted how Mochuda cursed the men of Fir Cell for denying him hospitality, and pronounced a lay that cursed them to be slain like pigs, for their family to be luckless and short-lived, for their women to be lustful and wanton, and for their house to be without prosperity or progeny.

1 Although often used for magical purposes, the black fast itself was an orthodox Christian fasting, and the word 'black' merely denotes its severe nature.

On another occasion, when king Blathmac led a company of men to forcibly expel the saint from his monastery, Mochuda cursed one man to death and another with dysentery. And, when one of the king's men winked at Mochuda mockingly, the saint cursed him so the offending eye remained forever closed, and his mouth fixed in a permanent grin. Mochuda declared this accursed affliction should be passed onto each of his descendants.

Eventually the king's men managed to expel Mochuda from his monastery, but on reaching a cross the saint turned to curse one of the men who had forcibly evicted him, saying, "may the hand that you laid upon me be accursed and the face you turned against me to expel me from my home be repulsive and scrofulous for the remainder of your life." Mochuda's curse was granted, and the man's eye was thereupon destroyed in his head. Finally, the saint turned to the king and pronounced a curse upon him:

> Behold the heavens above you and the earth below. Heaven you may not possess and even from your earthly principality may you soon be driven. And your brother, whom you have reproached because he would not lay hands on me, shall possess it instead of you, and in your lifetime. You shall be despised by all—so much so that in your brother's house they shall forget to supply you with food. Moreover yourself and your children shall come to an evil end and in a little while there shall not be one of your seed remaining.

As Mochuda cursed the king, he 'rang his small bell against him and against his race', and true to the saint's word, despite Blathmac's numerous progeny, his race was entirely wiped out. The bell thereafter became known as *The Bell of Blathmac's Extinguishing*, or *The Bell of Blathmac's Drowning*, because it drowned or extinguished the king and his posterity.

A particularly interesting element of Mochuda's curse is the ringing of the bell. The practice of ringing a bell whilst making an invocation, malediction, or blessing is found cross-culturally, and is typically used to draw attention to the spoken formulae within the magico-religious rite. The bell's knoll thus serves to underscore and affirm the saint's blessing or curse, and is effectively synonymous with the binding sentence pronounced at the end of a spell or prayer, such as Amen, Fiat, and So Be It.

Saints often carried small 'miracle-working' bells, and surviving exemplars were frequently revered as holy relics possessing preternatural power. Examples include St. Patrick's Bell Shrine, St. Conall Cael's Bell Shrine, and the medieval Irish Bell Shrine of St. Cuileáin, the latter of which is housed in the British Museum. Whilst the bells of the saints had many powers, those used to declare curses were oft described as having an 'ill-omened' or 'calamitous' nature.[2] St. Maedoc, who is renowned for hurling a great number of curses, made frequent reference to the imprecatory use of relics and bells, and on one occasion declared:

> Woe to him against whom my bells utter voice; woe to him against whom my bells are rung every morning and every evening.[3]

Herein, St. Maedoc essentially declared the power of the bell's knoll to be synonymous with the power of the speech act. On another occasion he avowed:

> Whoever they be against whom my bells are rung, they are destroyed and killed by them. The voice of my sanctuary and my relics places souls in hell.[4]

The exaction of such curses through the sounding of bells perhaps relates to the 'cursing ritual' of excommunication, which is colloquially referred to as the rite of 'bell, book, and candle' on account of its ceremony being punctuated by the ringing of a bell. The use of bells to repel wicked sinners is also commensurate to the folk belief in its power to drive away ghosts, evil spirits, witches, the devil, and the evil eye.

Bells were also amongst the maledictive techniques employed in the

2 Lester K. Little, *Benedictine Maledictions*, p. 169.

3 Charles Plummer, *Lives of Irish Saints*, p. 276.

4 Ibid., 277.

'Curse of Tara', which was exacted by St. Ruadhán, who fasted, sang 'the psalms of commination' (the imprecatory Psalms), and rang his bell against king Diarmuid. This curse resulted in the death of the sons of Tara's twelve kings, who had been placed in Diarmuid's care. A copper alloy bell allegedly belonging to St. Ruadhán is now housed in the British Museum.[5]

Another example of imprecatory bell-ringing concerns St. Maignenn, whose clerics rang their bells whilst uttering curses against a thief who had stolen a cow from a leper in Kilmainham.

A rather less successful attempt to use a bell to curse and repel evil concerns the 5th Century saint, St. Patrick. Whilst the saint fasted and prayed atop the summit of *Croagh Patrick* (County Mayo) for the 40 days of lent, he was harassed and tormented by demons who had taken

5 Museum Number 1854,0714.1; The British Museum, London.

the form of a cloud of blackbirds, which nefarious merle was so dense they turned the sky black. To disperse the birds, St. Patrick sang cursing psalms (*gabais salmu escaine foraib*) and loudly rang his bell at them, but they continued to plague him. In frustration he threw his bell at them, but missed, and when the bell hit the earth it split asunder. As the saint cried in despair an angel came down, and taking pity on him it turned the blackbirds into white songbirds.

Cursing saints are also found outside Britain. Illustrative is St. Bertrand, the 12th Century bishop of Comminges (France), who employed both liturgical excommunications and general curses in his pursuit of punishing wrongdoers. When a knight kidnapped a man under Bertrand's protection and refused to release him, the captor was struck with, 'an affliction in his eyes, sent from heaven, as if the mark of Cain were imprinted on his eyelids'. Eventually the recalcitrant knight released the captive, albeit unwillingly. On another occasion an adulterous woman who swore a false oath of innocence before St. Bertrand had her hand withered up, and a priest who refused to acquiesce to the saint's orders to correct his sexual behaviour had his house cursed, which caused it to collapse.[6]

The curses meted out by saints often took their inspiration from the Bible, for which reason the calamities visited upon their victims included disease, plague, the withering of limbs, death, loss of home and land, and the cursing of the victim's descendants (i.e., a 'generational curse'). In this way the lives and actions of the saints came to evoke those of the biblical prophets, thus promoting the idea the saints were the spiritual successors of the scriptural prophets.

However, some of the maledictions hurled by the saints demonstrate very little similarity to biblical exemplars, and these more colourful and creative methods of cursing are thought to originate in native folk traditions. It is also notable that many of the saints' imprecatory powers, such as making the land barren, withering limbs, and causing people to become paralysed or fixed to the spot, are also firmly associated with witchcraft and the evil eye.

One example of a biblically-inspired malediction is the generational curse pronounced by St. Malarchy of Armagh in the 1140s, which was

6 Robert Bartlett, *Why Can the Dead Do Such Great Things?*, pp. 402–3.

directed at the nobleman Robert de Brus 2nd and all his future descendants. The curse was occasioned when de Brus chose to hang a thief that Malarchy had asked to be pardoned, even though the nobleman had initially agreed to the saint's request. Soon after the curse was pronounced, de Brus 'died a wretched death', and three of his heirs were successively 'snatched away in the first flower of their age.' Nearly two hundred years later in 1319, one of de Brus's descendants, Robert de Brus 5th, sought to lift the generational curse by visiting St. Malarchy's tomb every two years to pray for forgiveness. He also endowed the tomb with monies for three silver lamps using funds gained whilst crusading in the Holy Lands with the soon-to-be Edward I:

> Charter by Robert de Brus, Lord of Annandale, granting to God and Blessed Mary and the house and monks of Clairvaux, in order to maintain lights before the blessed Malarchy and for the good of his own soul and the souls of his predecessors and successors...

As a result of this votive act, he 'made perpetual peace with the Saint', and lived into his seventies.

The cursing of a victim's land is particularly common in the hagiographies. One example is the malediction uttered by St. Laisrech, who condemned the lands of those who refused her tribute, turning them to nettles, elder shrub, and corncrakes. Another is the curse St. Eogan pronounced against a chieftain who denied him hospitality, which caused the chieftain's land to become barren and his fort to be lost. Expounding upon St. Eogan's power, his hagiographer wrote, 'whatever the man of God blessed was blessed, and whatever he cursed, his curse was enough for it.' Waters could also be cursed, as demonstrated by the malediction St. Patrick laid on the river Dub when some fisherman refused him any of their catch. On another occasion the Irish saint cursed the Oengae and Séle because two of his disciples drowned in them.[7]

7 Lisa M. Bitel, 'Saints and Angry Neighbours; The Politics of Cursing in Irish Hagiography' in *Monks & Nuns, Saints & Outcasts; Religion in Medieval Society* edited by Lester K. Little, pp. 140–1.

The hagiographies are also replete with tales of saints visiting disability and disease upon their victims. Illustrative is the malediction St. Aiden cast to repel some Anglo-Saxon raiders, which caused them to go blind for a whole year. Another example is the malediction St. Mochuda pronounced upon a beggar who tried to falsely claim alms by closing his eyes under the pretence he was blind, which curse permanently blinded the charlatan. Another tale concerns St. Máedóc, who invoked Jesus to curse those who violated his property, declaring, "Five diseases the Son of God inflicts on those whom I excommunicate or who outrage me: consumption, cholera, paralysis, sudden death, and hell." This example demonstrates how excommunication not only separated a victim from the church, but also had the power to afflict bodily ailments and secure the excommunicant's untimely death.

A particularly colourful malediction is found in the *Life of Columba*, and concerns a priest named Findchan, who abetted the ordination of Aid the Black as priest, despite the fact this Cruthinian-of-royal-descent had been a bloodthirsty murderer. Findchan was greatly attached to Aid 'in a carnal way' and gave his mark of approval for the ordination of this questionable candidate by placing his right hand upon the sinner's head in front of a bishop. When St. Columba heard of Findchan's sponsorship of Aid's ordination he pronounced a mighty curse on the priest, saying

> That right hand which, contrary to divine law and the law of the church, Findchan has laid upon the head of a son of perdition will presently rot, and after torments of great pain will precede him into the earth in burial; and surviving after his hand has been buried he will live for many years. And Aid, thus irregularly ordained, shall return as a dog to his vomit, and be again a bloody murderer, until at length, pierced in the neck with a spear, he shall fall from a tree into water and be drowned.

St. Columba's curse soon came to pass. Findchan's right hand began to fester, and eventually had to be cut off and buried, although he himself lived many years thereafter. Aid the Black also met his decreed fate, and after returning to his evil ways he suffered the promised triple-death;

after being treacherously wounded with a spear he fell from the prow of a boat into a lake and was drowned.

The hagiographies are replete with hand-withering curses. Exemplars include the hand-withering curse St. Cóemgen cast at a foster-mother for striking St. Colmán Ela, the hand-withering curse St. Mannu directed against some soldiers who tried to kill a hostage he requested be spared, and the hand-withering curse cast at a jealous monk who made an attempt on the life of St. Máedoc.

Another malediction popular with the saints was the paralysis or freezing of a victim, whereby the curse was cast with and without spoken formulae. For example, when St. Faenche, sister of St. Énna, prayed for retribution against some bandits, they were struck with paralysis, and were only released from their curse after they repented. St. Faenche's hagiographer explained her powers by referring to *Matthew* 16:19, 'Whatever you shall bind on earth, shall be bound in heaven.' Herein the saint's power to magically enchant and release a victim by heavenly power was given biblical basis, further fostering the belief in the saints as spiritual successors of the biblical prophets.

The Cursing Clergy

THe Christian cursing tradition, as established by scripture and hagiography, found continued nourishment in the bosom of 'the Church', whose ambivalence to cursing is evident in the maledictions its ecclesiasts hurled against those engaging in undesirable behaviours, or who worked against God and his appointed earthly representatives. In making such imprecations, the clergy were following a convention predicated upon scriptural episodes wherein God's prophets cursed those wrongdoers who opposed or mocked the Lord, His teachings, or His earthly representatives. Because such clerical maledictions were in line with Biblical teaching, they were generally deemed licit by state and church. Illustrative of this scriptural antecedent are the words of Moses, who said:

> Behold, I set before you this day a blessing and a curse; A blessing, if ye obey the commandments of the Lord your

> God, which I command you this day: And a curse, if ye will not obey the commandments of the Lord your God. (*Deuteronomy* 11:26–28)

The Council of Aachen reiterated this Mosaic precept in 837, expressing their conviction that, 'those who obey the divine precepts deserve a benediction, while those who disobey them deserve a malediction.' It was believed such priestly curses had great power when motivated by just cause, as confirmed by a writer in 1659, who declared, 'where God bids curse, there is cause to fear cursing'.[8]

When it comes to spiritous intercession and magic, it is often said there is no black or white magic—no good or evil—there is just power. Indeed, when it comes to the practicalities of magic, one single act of power may be viewed as black or white, good or evil, dependent upon the manner in which it affects the person(s). Typically, powers and magic benefitting an individual or group are deemed 'good', whilst those that work against them are deemed 'evil'. As a result, curses uttered by clerics to bolster the security of the Church and its faithful were generally considered licit and 'good', whilst those threatening the security of the Church—such as the imprecations hurled by lay-folk and non-Christians—were deemed illicit, evil, and the work of the devil.

Aside from 'tradition', the clergy's authority to curse is also founded upon a recognition of the Church's appointed ministers as intercessors and conduits for God's power. If God bestows His blessing upon those things His clergy have pronounced blessings over, then it follows He might equally curse those things they have pronounced curses over. This is to say, just as the priest's blessing serves to make a thing holy, and thereby raise it up to the heavens, so does the priest's malediction serve to make a thing accursed, and cast it down to hell. These twain priestly powers are codified in the motif of St. Peter's crossed keys, which symbolise the power to open the gates of heaven and hell. Herein the words of the priest are shown to have a power beyond that of merely communicating information, and actually have an ability to cause the change in circumstance that their words express, whether to consecrate objects,

8 C. Burges, *No Sacrifice nor Sinne to Aliene or Purchase the Lands of the Bishops* (2nd edition, 1659), p. 174.

bind people in holy union, free them of original sin, bless them, excommunicate them, or curse them. Comparable is the power of the magus to cause change in conformity with will, which is similarly expressed through vocal ejaculation and ritual action.

As God's ministers were considered conduits for His power, the formidable curses delivered by them were much feared by the populace. Such curses, and the fear of them, were particularly useful during the medieval period, when monks, canons, and the like could not rely upon the state or physical strength to protect themselves and their property.

It was commonly believed the saints looked after the church within which they were enshrined, and would punish those who stole or vandalised the church's property, or harmed the saint's servants. To this end, when ecclesiasts made maledictions to protect themselves and their property, they would frequently appeal to their patron saint. For example, in the *Miracles of St. Bavo* it is told how a knight trampled some crops whilst chasing a young hare. Aggrieved, a servant of the saint said, "Alas, St. Bavo, why do you not defend your field?" No sooner had he spoken, than the knight fell and broke his hip, and so too did the hare stumble and break its neck.

Also, when Picot, the sheriff of Cambridgeshire, ordered his wicked servant, Gervase, to oppress and harass the 'the men of St. Etheldreda', the Abbot instructed his religious community to sing the seven penitential Psalms before the holy virgin's tomb to beg for aid. In answer to their prayers, the spirit of St. Etheldreda appeared before Gervase at night, and after rebuking him for the persecution of her men, she stabbed him through the heart with her staff. The wounded tyrant lived only long enough to tell of the saint's vengeful visitation.

Like their priestly brethren, monks were also considered religious virtuosos capable of wielding divine power for the purposes of blessing and cursing. Indeed, tales abound of monks hurling ruinous imprecations against their enemies with great gusto, and like the priest's curse these maledictions were greatly feared by the common folk, for they had the power of God behind them.

Illustrative of the power invested in the monk's curse is a case from Gerald of Wales' *Topographia Hibernica* (c. 1188). In 1185 Hugh Tyrell and Philip of Worcester invaded a monastery and forced the monks to hand over a large hoard of valuable goods, amongst which was a prized bronze cooking pot, which Tyrell determined to take as his own. Angered by this act of larceny, the monks hurled curses at the raiders as they left the monastery. These maledictions seemingly had their effect, because that night a fire broke out in the building where the cauldron was stored, which destroyed the building, most of the settlement, and the two horses used to haul away the ill-gotten gains. The cooking pot alone remained undamaged, and when Tyrell beheld this, he felt guilty and returned it to the monks. However, his repentance was not enough to assuage the curse, and the bishop of Louth predicted that Tyrell would "this year certainly meet with a grievous misfortune. Never was it known that the tears and curses of so many good men were spent in vain." Sure enough, before the year was out, Tyrell became inexplicably embroiled in a violent quarrel with his good friend, Hugo de Lacy, which conflict caused great sorrow for many years.

A particularly well-known malediction incepted by the ire of a monk is the 'curse of the Coburgs'. In 1816 the Coburg prince, Ferdinand, married a Hungarian princess named Antoinette de Kohary, who was the only child of Prince Joseph de Kohary and the sole heir of her father's vast fortune. However, one of Antoinette's poorer relatives, a Hungarian monk named Brother Emericus Kohary, was envious of this bequest. It is said he went to a churchyard in Darmstadt at midnight, where he arranged a circle of candles, and stood therein and solemnly read out a curse according to the ritual of the *Manuale Exorcisorum*, saying, "Then verily shall I pray to the Lord Almighty to visit the sins of the fathers upon the children to the third and fourth generation of the Coburg line." Thereafter, great misfortune plagued the Coburg family, and whilst they were beset with typhoid fever, death during childbirth, suicide, and other great hardships, 'the curse of the Coburgs' is most commonly associated with hæmophilia, which illness claimed the lives of many Coburgs and those inheriting its line.

The maledictions used by ecclesiasts broadly fall into four types, namely prayer curses, liturgical maledictions, clamours, and excommunications.

Imprecatory Prayer

IMprecatory prayer is essentially the act of petitioning God and his holy retinue to bring divine retribution to bear upon an individual or group. Although the prayer's content was generally left to individual ingenium, many took the lead of the Saints and drew upon biblical sources for inspiration.

One example of an informal imprecatory prayer concerns the 'curse of Maesyfelin'. Maesyfelin was a stately mansion that stood upon the banks of the river Dulas near Lampeter, home to the Lloyd family. Around the beginning of the 17th Century there was a dispute between Sir Francis Lloyd of Maesyfelin and Samuel Pritchard, who was the son of the vicar of Llandovery. This quarrel, allegedly over an illicit love affair, resulted in the brutal murder of Samuel, whose body was carried by night to the river Towy (Carmarthenshire) and consigned to the watery depths. When the body was later discovered, Samuel's grieving father pronounced a curse on Maesyfelin, saying:

> Melldith Duw ar Maesyfelin!
> Ar bob carreg, ar bob gwreiddyn,
> Am daflu blodau tref Llan'ddyfri,
> Ar ei ben i Dywi i foddi.
>
> (The curse of God on Maesyfelin!
> On every stone, and root therein,
> For throwing the flower of Llandovery town,
> To Towy's water, there to drown.)

As a result of the vicar's curse, God's judgement befell the family and mansion of Maesyfelin, causing their fortune to diminish and their house to fall into ruin. Debris from the ruins were later taken to repair the nearby mansion of Peterwell, and when this place also fell into ruin it was believed the curse had been carried there upon the accursed rocks of Maesyfelin.

Liturgical Malediction

LIke liturgical benedictions, liturgical maledictions followed prescribed forms, and were typically read out during community worship, which served to make the curse public. Although there were no *maledictionals* to compliment the *benedictionals* containing the clerical formulas used for making divine blessings, such imprecatory rites are sometimes found written in Bibles, books of prayer, and other religious texts.

Liturgical maledictions took much of their inspiration from scripture, as illustrated by this 10th Century exemplar from the Abbey of Féfchamp:

> We curse them and we separate them from the company of the holy mother church and of all faithful Christians,
> Unless they change their ways and give back what they unjustly took away...
> May they be cursed in the head and the brain.
> May they be cursed in their eyes and their foreheads.
> May they be cursed in their ears and their noses.
> May they be cursed in fields and in pastures...
> May they be cursed when sleeping and when awake, when going out and returning, when eating and drinking, when speaking and being silent.
> May they be cursed in all places at all times.[9]

Like many liturgical curses, this malediction borrows heavily from *Deuteronomy* 28. Another 10th Century liturgical curse drawing upon *Deuteronomy* 28 was found inscribed in a Bible at the Abbey of Saint-Martial of Limoges (France), and was pronounced against men who were 'devastating the land of our lord Martial':

9 Lester Little, *Benedictine Maledictions*, p. 9.

May they be cursed and excommunicated and anathematised and separated from the consortium of all the faithful Christians of God.
May the curse of all the saints of God come upon them.
May the angels and archangels of God curse them.
May the patriarchs and the prophets curse them.
May all the apostles and all the martyrs and all the confessors and all the virgins and especially, Saint Martial, whom they are treating so badly, curse them.
May he confound and destroy them, and disperse them from the face of the earth.
May all these curses come upon them and seize them.

May they be cursed in town; May they be cursed in the fields.
May they be cursed inside their houses, and outside their houses.
May they be cursed sitting and standing.
May they be cursed lying down and walking.
May they be cursed when asleep and when awake.
May they be cursed when eating and drinking.
May they be cursed in castles and in villages.
May they be cursed in forests and in waters.

May their wives and the children and all who associate with them be cursed.
May their cellars be cursed, as well as their casks and all the vessels from which they eat and drink.
May their vineyards and their crops and their forests be cursed.
May their servants, if they remain loyal to them, be cursed.
May all their cattle and their work animals, both inside and outside the stables, be cursed.
May the Lord send over them hunger and thirst, pestilence and death, until they are wiped off the earth.
May the Lord strike them with heat and with cold.
May the sky above them be brass and the earth they walk on iron.
May the Lord toss their bodies as bait to the birds of the sky and the beasts of the land.

May the Lord strike them from the bottom of their feet to the top of their heads.
May their homes be deserted and may no one inhabit them.
May they lose what they have and may they not acquire what they do not have.
May the sword devastate them on the outside and fear on the inside.
If they sow seeds on the earth, may they reap little, and if they plant vines, may they not drink wine from them.
May the Lord send great plagues upon them, and the worst, most relentless illnesses, unless they change their ways.
But if they are not willing to change, then let them accept from God and Saint Martial damnation with the devil and his angels in hell, and may they burn in eternal fires with Sathan and Abiron.
Amen, amen.

Thus may all memory of them be extinguished forever and ever.

This curse from the Abbey of Saint-Martial of Limoges is fairly representative of liturgical maledictions, which typically contained the following elements:

The naming of the offending parties, and a declaration of what they have done to warrant the curse.

An enumeration of the various spiritous agencies being entreated to exact the curse. For example, 'May the angels and archangels curse them, May the patriarchs and the prophets curse them...'

A description of the curse, specifically where they are to be cursed, and the effect(s) the curse is to have, e.g., 'may they be cursed sitting and standing...may the Lord send over them hunger and thirst.' By detailing a comprehensive miscellany of situations the individual is to be cursed in ('sitting and standing', 'sleeping and waking' etc.) the curse is effectively rendered inescapable.

Whilst the malediction strikes the victim first, the verbal formula articulates an intent for it to spread outwards, like an infection, thereby affecting those around the accursed individual, i.e., their family, friends, and servants. However, should these unfortunate souls cease to associate with the individual, they are freed of the curse. Through this mechanism the malediction seeks to divorce the accursed individual from their family and community, thereby isolating them.

Maledictions often included an escape clause allowing for the curse to be rendered ineffective if the victim should amend their ways. Herein the curse is shown to be a coercive device intended to pressure the individual into changing their ways, which illustrates how those casting liturgical maledictions saw themselves as rightful enforcers of the Divine will.

Maledictions typically ended with a binding phrase, such as 'amen' (meaning 'so be it'), to seal the curse.

Another liturgical rite calling upon God to intercede, pronounce judgment, and deliver punishment was the Judgement Mass, which, although widely practiced, was nonetheless considered an abuse in the eyes of the Church. The Mass of Judgment is predicated upon the principles underpinning the 'waters of jealousy' rite, also known as 'the ordeal of the bitter waters', which is found in *Numbers* 5:11–31 and purportedly established whether a man's wife was innocent or guilty of infidelity.

In 'the ordeal of the bitter waters' the wife was presented to a priest and given an earthenware cup containing holy water mixed with holy dust taken from the floor of the tabernacle. The charges against her were spoken, and she was told that if she were innocent she had nothing to fear from drinking the 'bitter waters'. However, if she was guilty the drink would go into her bowels and cause her 'belly to swell and her thigh to rot', and she would be a curse amongst the people. The priest wrote the words of this curse onto a scroll and blotted them into the water, thereby causing the words of the curse to infuse the philter. This deed effectively produced a liquid curse, whose bitter waters the woman drank that God's judgement would be revealed by her fate.

This rite pre-supposes written curses to have an inherent power capable of being passed into other things through contact and contagion. The tradition of immersing written charms in water to infuse the liquid with the concomitant power is one that later obtained in folk magic. Indeed, in the early 20th Century a Norfolk doctor recounted how a bewitched woman attempted to lift her curse by writing the Lord's Prayer on a piece of paper, soaking it in water until the ink ran, and then drinking the infused water.[10]

A curse similar to the 'waters of jealousy' rite, albeit aimed at discovering a thief, is found within the *Black Books of Elverum* (c. 1800), which handwritten grimoires were found in an attic in Norway. The operant is to write the following words on a piece of cheese using alum water (a solution of mineral salts):

Max, Pax, Firax.

Or else this incantation, which contains distorted fragments of Latin liturgy:

Neguba, Exgvieda arrears Finte am Tuam Tasie dollore.

The Lord's Prayer is then read over the cheese on three Sundays whilst fasting, but never saying Amen. The cheese is afterwards given to the suspected thief, and if he is guilty he will immediately throw up.[11]

Like the 'ordeal by bitter waters', the Mass of Judgement also brought issues of wrongdoing before God, who was left to make judgement and dispense punishment where warranted. Moreover, in both rites the accused, in agreeing to the rite and making the oath, effectively invokes their own curse when judged guilty.

To prepare for the Mass of Judgement, the accused went to the priest three days before the trial's appointed date, and thereafter fasted on bread, herbs, salt, and water. They also assisted the priest and made offerings at Mass. During the third day's Mass, just before Communion, the accused was brought before the altar and adjured by their love of

10 Michael Howard, *East Anglian Witches and Wizards*, p. 146.

11 Mary Rustad, *The Black Books of Elverum*, pp. 61–3.

God, their faith, the regenerative force of their baptism, and by the power of the holy relics housed in the church, that they should only receive the Eucharist and submit to the forthcoming ordeal if they were truly innocent. If the accused chose to go ahead, the priest gave them the Holy Communion, saying, "May this Body and Blood of Our Lord Jesus Christ prove thee innocent or guilty this day."

When the Mass had finished, the accused once again affirmed their innocence by making an oath, saying, "In the Lord I am guiltless, both in word and deed, of the crime of which I am accused." They were then led to the trial, which took one of four forms:

> A priest said a prayer over a small barley cake, asking that the accused, if guilty, be made pale and shaky on receiving the cake, for their jaw to seize up and be unable to chew, for their throat to contract and refuse to swallow, and for the cake to be expelled from their mouth. The cake was then given to the accused individual, who was watched for any such signs of guilt. Comparable are the physical signs watched for after drinking the 'waters of jealousy'.

> The accused was stripped, bound hand and foot, sprinkled with holy water, and given a cross and book of gospels to kiss. They were then tied about the waist with a long cord and thrown into a body of water. If the accused sank they were deemed innocent and immediately liberated, but if they floated they were judged guilty and handed over to the officers of justice. This trial is one to which suspected witches were commonly subjected.

> In a remote part of the church, a fire was kindled beneath a water-filled cauldron, and a stone or piece of iron was placed within. Litanies were then said, and once the water reached boiling point the accused was commanded to put their bare arm into the water and remove the stone or lump of iron. The priest then wrapped the accused's arm in clean linen and fixed it with the seal of the church. After three days the arm was un-bandaged and if the wound

had not perfectly healed the accused was deemed guilty. It is difficult to imagine how those accused had any chance of being found innocent by this method.

A fire was kindled in a remote part of the church, and once the Mass was begun a one to three-pound iron bar was placed on the hot coals. At the end of the Mass the scalding bar was taken off the coals and placed on a small stone pillar. The accused was then challenged to pick up the iron bar, take three steps, and throw it down. As before, the scalded hand was bandaged and checked three days later, with an imperfectly healed wound being considered a sure sign of guilt.

In some continental nations a fifth ordeal was added, which took the form of a duel or private battle.[12]

Writing on the Judgement Mass, Dr Lingard in his *History of the Antiquities of the Anglo-Saxon Church (1806)* suggests that just as the Anglo-Saxons had once entrusted difficult judgements regarding justice and prosecution to 'the wisdom of Woden', so too did they expect the same miraculous intercession from God after their conversion to Christianity. He also remarks how the Mass of Judgement is found amongst all northern nations embracing Christianity after the 5th Century, being practiced by both barbaric and civilised societies alike. For example, St. Cunegunda, the virginal wife of King Henry II of Germany, proved herself innocent of adultery by this method, and went through the ordeal of walking over several red-hot ploughshares entirely unhurt. However, the Judgement Mass was condemned by various authorities, including Pope Gregory the Great in 592 CE, the Council of Worms in 829 CE, and Pope Nicholas 1 in 858 CE.

Liturgical maledictions also took the form of masses pronounced against enemies of the Church and state. For example, in 1589, the Sorbonne University of Paris sanctioned a series of masses directed against King Henri III.[13] An earlier example are the *contra paganos* prayers and

12 John Lingard, *History of the Antiquities of the Anglo-Saxon Church*, pp. 184–6.

13 Miri Rubin, *Corpus Christi; The Eucharist in Late Medieval Culture*, p. 338.

masses favoured by the Anglo-Saxons, which emerged in the 9th Century as a type of votive mass to call upon God's help in defeating pagan opposition, especially that from 'the Northmen'. Some of these simply asked God to crush and repel the enemy, but others included imprecatory Psalms for delivery from enemies, passages likening the army of the Christian ruler to the hosts of Israel, and comparisons made to the conflict between David and Goliath. The latter were in essence narrative charms appealing to God for magical aid, as with the entreaty 'just as you helped the Israelites, so too may you help us.' Historically, peoples beseeching God to smite their oppressors and opponents have often compared themselves and their suffering to the people of Israel, God's 'chosen people', and in so doing likened their own adversaries to the enemies of the ancient Hebrews, and thus the enemies of God.

The *contra paganus* Votive Mass was not only used to vanquish 'pagans', but was later employed against heretics and those of a non-Christian religious faith. For example, during the Crusades this mass was used against the Saracens. During the 20th Century the *contra paganus* mass was retitled as the *pro ecclesiæe defensions* ('for the defence of the Church'), ostensibly to shift its emphasis from being an act of aggression into an act of defence, and was authorised for use against any enemy of the Church. However, this shift in emphasis was purely superficial, as the wording of the rite was left unchanged, still asking that 'the pagan nations who trust in their own ferocity may be crushed by the power of God's right hand, and that those who fight for us may escape all pagan snares and perils.' This phraseology served to define all enemies of the church as 'pagan', regardless of their faith, thereby lumping them into one adversarial and devilish 'other' against which the Church could fight. This pejorative use of the word 'pagan' also worked to further cement the word's association with wickedness and impiety in the minds of the Christian populace.

The Clamour

OF itself, the clamour is not a curse, but rather a vigorous appeal to God and His holy retinue—the apostles, confessors, and saints—for preternatural aid. However, when such petitions are made against an enemy the clamour *de facto* becomes an imprecation. For example, when a knight named Hilouin was pillaging the Abbey of Marchiennes (Flanders), the monks let out their clamours whilst ringing their bells and hurling anathemas. A year then passed, and at the very hour of the clamour's anniversary the plundering knight Hilouin fell down dead. Moreover, because churches and religious communities were considered to be under the protective auspices of the saint in whose name they were founded, it was to these patron saints their incumbents frequently turned when seeking to overcome an enemy or threat.

Fortunately, a number of written formulas for making clamours survive, along with instruction as to the various ritualistic acts to be performed, which include standing, kneeling, ringing bells, and extinguishing candles. In all, there are over sixty known examples, dating from the 10th to the 13th century. These are mostly contained in liturgical books and are entitled as a *clamour ad deum* ('clamour to God') or simply *maledictio*.[14]

Whilst clamours typically took the form of supplicatory petitions, in extreme cases the priesthood attempted to cajole the saints into action by humiliating them. This act of degradation was accomplished by removing crucifixes, sacred texts, holy relics, and hallowed icons from their altars or places of exaltation, and placing them upon the ground before the altar, sometimes on a piece of rough cloth. In some cases, the holy objects were also covered with a veil so no-one could gaze upon them, and the church doors were barred with thorns. It was believed the saints, riled by their humiliation, were thus goaded into directing their wrath at those who had provoked the priesthood to take such extreme action. These deeds were essentially a form of blackmail, for it was implicit the saint's hallowed icons would only be returned to their exalted and venerated position if he or she kept their end of the deal, protecting and providing for the religious community.

The making of clamours is illustrated by a case from 1197, which is preserved in Roger of Howden's 12th Century *Chronicle*, and concerns John Cumin, the archbishop of Dublin, who wished to force the King to address his grievances. In order to obtain preternatural aid in the

14 Lester Little, 'The Separation of Religious Curses from Blessings in the Latin West', p. 30.

fulfilment of his wish, the archbishop placed the crosses and images of the cathedral church upon the floor amidst thorns, which he vowed to leave there until the situation had been resolved. Amongst the holy icons was a much-venerated crucifix that bore 'an expressive figure of Christ'. After six days laying prostrate, the figure began to show signs of torment—its face reddened and tears fell from its eyes—miraculous signs that were considered redolent of the agonies suffered on the cross.

Clamours were commonly made whilst kneeling or laying prostrate on the floor, which posture betrays the stance of humility necessary for the supplicant to approach a sainted spirit. However, some suggest these gestures also served as a symbolic humiliation and defilement of the ordained minister—and thus a humiliation of God and his holy retinue—which was intended to further provoke the saint's ire and his or her desire for revenge.

Despite their popularity, desecratory clamours were not entirely licit, and in the seventeenth constitution of the 1274 meeting of the Second Council of Lyons, the council fathers condemned such behaviour:

> ...[we] utterly rebuke the detestable abuse and horrible impiety of those who treating with irreverent boldness crucifixes and images or statues of the blessed Virgin and other saints, throw them to the ground in order to emphasise the suspension of divine worship, and leave them under nettles and thorns. We forbid severely any sacrilege of this kind. We decree that those who disobey are to receive a hard retributive sentence, which will so chastise the offenders as to suppress the like arrogance in others.

Excommunication and Anathema

EXcommunication and anathema are perhaps the most well-known of the ecclesiastical maledictions. Excommunication varied in its severity, ranging from minor excommunication, which prohibited the individual from receiving the sacrament, to major excommunication, which divorced the individual from the church entirely. In some instances, major excommunication also prohibited people

from social intercourse with Christian folk, and where a community was predominantly Christian this included the victim's kith and kin, which effectively constituted complete societal ostracism.

Major excommunication is sometimes known as *anathema*, and was usually reserved for heresy and other grave 'crimes'. In 1672 the French Jesuit, Jacques Eveillon, published a book on excommunication and anathema that expounded upon the difference between the two:

> Anathema augments the punishments of excommunication beyond what simple excommunication does, such that the anathematised is more deprived of the protection of God, and more absolutely exposed and abandoned to the rage and violence of this furious enemy, and by virtue of the maledictions that the church pronounces against him; and for the same reasons is called in the canons of excommunication *maledictus*...The maledictions that are usually pronounced in a sentence of anathema are not used in an ordinary and simple excommunication.[15]

In the medieval period, major excommunication typically involved a solemn ritual carried out by a bishop and twelve priests (evoking Christ and His apostles), who gathered together in a conspicuous place, each holding a lit candle. The rite concluded with the following words:

> Wherefore in the name of God the All-powerful, Father, Son, and Holy Ghost, of the Blessed Peter, Prince of the Apostles, and of all the saints, in virtue of the power which has been given us of binding and loosing in Heaven and on earth, we deprive him and all his accomplices and all his abettors of the Communion of the Body and Blood of Our Lord, we separate him from the society of all Christians, we exclude him from the bosom of our Holy Mother the Church in Heaven and on earth, we declare him excommunicated and anathematised and we judge him condemned to eternal fire with Satan and his angels

15 Ibid., 37–8.

> and all the reprobate, so long as he will not burst the fetters of the demon, do penance and satisfy the Church; we deliver him to Satan to mortify his body, that his soul may be saved on the day of judgment.

After this the priests responded, "Fiat, fiat, fiat", meaning 'so be it, so be it, so be it.' The bishop then rang a bell, which declared the public nature of the act and evoked the spectre of the death knell, closed a holy book, which represented the separation of the excommunicant from the church, and snuffed out the candle(s) by casting them to the floor and treading them underfoot. This trinity of concluding acts gave rise to the colloquialism, 'by bell, book, and candle.' After the rite, written notice was given to the neighbouring clergy to ensure they knew the victim(s) had been excommunicated and why.

The treatment of the candle in the excommunication rite is symbolic in nature, with the candle serving as a proxy for the victim, and its manipulation evoking the terrible effect the excommunication was to have upon them. As the candle was blown out, the victim's soul was cast into darkness and removed from God's Light, and as it was thrown to the floor it was cast down to earth and away from God's sight. This deed recalls the belief that just as ascent is a sign of exaltation, so too is descent is one of condemnation. This is exemplified in the casting of the fallen angels from heaven to earth, and also the treatment of the souls of the dead: whilst the faithful are raised up to heaven, the damned are cast down into a hellish underworld.

This vengeful manipulation of the candle is commensurate to the execration of wax poppets and candles in folk magic, whereby the proxy of the victim is subjected to various deeds that, by language of analogy, demonstrate the magician's desire. To achieve such effect, the proxy is typically stabbed with pins, extinguished, bent, snapped, or trampled underfoot, even as the candle is so treated in the rite of excommunication.

Whilst major excommunication sought to ritually separate the individual from the bosom of the church, the rite itself was believed to have both a physical and a spiritual effect, which is to demonstrate the magical power of word. This is alluded to in the ritual's spoken formula, which articulates the deliverance of the victim to Satan that he might 'mortify his body.' Notably, many early anathemas call upon God to command the Devil to punish the victim, which implies a belief that the Devil is God's henchman, rather than an antithetical and autonomous principle of evil.

The power of excommunication to effect physical suffering is evinced in the declaration of St. Máedóc, who said, "Five diseases the Son of God inflicts on those whom I excommunicate or who outrage me: consumption, cholera, paralysis, sudden death and hell." Also, when the early 12th Century bishop of Comminges (France), excommunicated a man for building on land set aside for a burial ground, the excommunicant fell into a perpetual illness, which only abated when he amended his ways.

Where the offence was particularly heinous, the clergy would sometimes embellish the excommunication rite to the point it became tantamount to a ritualised curse, as illustrated by this example pronounced by Pope Benedict VIII in 1014:

> May they be cursed in the East, disinherited in the West, interdicted in the North, and excommunicated in the South.
>
> May they be cursed in the day and excommunicated at night.
>
> May they be cursed at home and excommunicated while away, cursed in standing and excommunicated in sitting...
>
> May they be cursed in the spring and excommunicated in the summer, cursed in the autumn and excommunicated in the winter.

Other excommunication curses were more succinct, such as "may they drain out through their bowels, like the faithless and unhappy Arius", and "may they be buried with dogs and asses, may rapacious wolves devour their cadavers."[16]

16 Little, *Benedictine Maledictions*, pp. 36, 47.

One of the most extensive early Christian curses is the Malediction of Bishop Ernulphus, which was an all-purpose curse that could be pronounced against an enemy. Ernulphus or Ernulf (1040–1124) was a Benedictine monk who was consecrated as Bishop of Rochester (England) in 1114. He was responsible for compiling the *Textus Roffensis*, which preserved various rites and rituals of Anglo-Saxon Christianity, including the rite of excommunication and damnation now named for him, even though it was already old by the time he recorded it:

The Malediction of Bishop Ernulphus

BY the authority of God Almighty, the Father, the Son, and Holy Ghost, and of the holy canons, and of the undefiled Virgin Mary, mother and patroness of our Saviour, and of all the celestial virtues, angels, archangels, thrones, dominions, powers, cherubims and seraphims, and of all the holy patriarchs, prophets, and of all the apostles and evangelists, and of the holy innocents, who in the sight of the Holy Lamb, are found worthy to sing the new song of the holy martyrs and holy confessors, and of the holy virgins, and of all the saints, together with the holy and elect of God.

We excommunicate and anathematise this malefactor, and from the thresholds of the holy church of God Almighty we sequester him, that he may be tormented, disposed and delivered over with Dathan and Abiram, and with those who say unto the Lord God, Depart from us, we desire none of thy ways. And as fire is quenched with water, so let the light of him be put out for evermore, unless it shall repent him and make satisfaction.

May the Father who created man, curse him.
May the Son who suffered for us, curse him.
May the Holy Ghost, who was given to us in baptism, curse him.

May the holy cross which Christ, for our salvation triumphing over his enemies, ascended, curse him.

May the holy and eternal Virgin Mary, mother of God, curse him.
May St Michael, the advocate of holy souls, curse him.
May all the angels and archangels, principalities and powers, and all the heavenly armies, curse him.
May St. John, the Praecursor, and St. John the Baptist, and St. Peter and Paul, and St. Andrew, and all the other Christ's apostles, together curse him.
And may the rest of his disciples and four evangelists, who by their preaching converted the universal world, and may the holy and wonderful company of martyrs and confessors, who by their holy works are found pleasing to God Almighty, curse him.

May the holy choir of the holy virgins, who for the honour of Christ have despised the things of the world, damn him.
May the saints, who from the beginning of the world to everlasting ages are found to be beloved of God, damn him.
May the heavens and earth, and all the holy things remaining in therein, damn him.

May he be damn'd wherever he be; whether in the house or the stables, the garden or the field, or the highway, or in the path, or in the wood, or in the water, or in the church.
May he be cursed in living, in dying.
May he be cursed in eating and drinking, in being hungry, in being thirsty, in fasting, in sleeping, in slumbering, in walking, in standing, in lying, in working, in resting, in pissing, in shitting, and in blood letting. May he be cursed in all the faculties of his body.
May he be cursed inwardly and outwardly!
May he be cursed in the hair of his head!

> May he be cursed in his brains, and in his vertex, in his temples, in his forehead, in his ears, in his eye-brows, in his cheeks, in his jaw-bones, in his nostrils, in his fore-teeth and grinders, in his lips, in his throat, in his shoulders, in his wrists, in his arms, in his hands, in his fingers!
> May he be damn'd in his mouth, in his breast, in his heart and purtenance, down to the very stomach!
> May he be cursed in his reins, and in his groin, in his thighs, in his genitals, and in his hips, and in his knees, his legs, and feet and toenails!
> May he be cursed in all the joints and articulations of his members, from the top of his head to the sole of his foot! May there be no soundness in him!
>
> May the Son of the living God, with all the Glory of his Majesty, curse him! And may heaven with all the powers that move therein, rise up against him, curse and damn him unless he repent and make satisfaction. Amen. So be it—so be it. Amen.

Perhaps the most dramatic and lengthy rite of excommunication was that pronounced by the Archbishop of Glasgow, Gavin Dunbar, circa 1524. It was made in response to the increasing lawlessness of the Anglo Scottish Borders, and sought to excommunicate the Border Reivers ('raiders'), so as to 'strike them with the terrible sword of the holy church, which they may not long endure or resist.' To this end he issued a lengthy Monition of Cursing against the Reivers, instructing all Border parish priests to read it to their congregations. This rite, which drew heavily from *Deuteronomy* 28, began with an appeal to divine authority to empower the curse:

> Herefore, through the authority of the Almighty God, the Father of heaven, his Son, our Saviour, Jesus Christ, and of the Holy Ghost; through the authority of the Blessed Virgin Saint Mary, Saint Michael, Saint Gabriel, and all his angels; Saint John the Baptist, and all the holy patriarchs and prophets; Saint Peter, Saint Paul, Saint Andrew, and

> all the holy apostles; Saint Stephen, Saint Laurence, and all the holy martyrs; Saint Gile, Saint Martin, and all the holy confessors; Saint Anne, Saint Katherine, and all holy virgins and matrons; and all the saints and holy company of heaven; by the authority of our Holy Father the Pope and his cardinals...

After this the curse proper begins, which being over 1,000 words is too lengthy to quote verbatim, but part of it runs as follows:

> I CURSE their head, and all the hairs of their head.
> I CURSE their face, their eyes, their mouth, their nose, their tongue, their teeth, their neck, their shoulders, their breast, their heart, their stomach, their back, their womb, their arms, their legs, their hands, their feet, and every part of their body, from the top of their head to the souls of their feet, before and behind, within and without.
> I CURSE them going, and I CURSE them riding;
> I CURSE them standing and I CURSE them sitting;
> I CURSE them eating, and I CURSE them drinking;
> I CURSE them waking, and I CURSE them sleeping;
> I CURSE them rising, and I CURSE them lying;
> I CURSE them at home, and I CURSE them from home;
> I CURSE them within the house, and I CURSE them without the house;
> I CURSE their wives, their children, and their servants who participate with them in their deeds.
>
> I WORRY their corn, their cattle, their wool, their sheep, their horse, their swine, their geese, their hens, and all their livestock.
> I WORRY their houses, their rooms, their kitchens, their stables, their barns, their byres, their barnyards, their vegetable patch, their ploughs, their harrows, and the goods and houses that are necessary for their sustenance and welfare.

> All the bad wishes and curses that ever befell a worldly creature since the beginning of the world to this hour might be upon them. The malediction of God, that lighted upon Lucifer and all his fellows, that struck them from the high heaven to the deep hell, might be upon them. The fire and the sword that stopped Adam from the gates of Paradise might stop them from the glory of Heaven until they forebear and make amends.

The malediction proceeds with an evocation of the various Biblical curses and punishments visited by God upon his enemies, including: the curse that lighted on Cain for slaying the guiltless Abel; the Flood that drowned the wicked; the thunder and lightning that rained down on Sodom and Gomorrah; the Plagues that afflicted Pharaoh and the Egyptians; all the plagues and pestilence that have ever been visited upon man and beast; and the maledictions that fell upon Absolom, Olifernus, Judas, Pilot, Herod, Simon Magus, the Jews who crucified Jesus, and all who have ever persecuted Christ's followers. The curse concludes with this final condemnation:

> And finally, I CONDEMN them perpetually to the deep pit of hell, to remain with Lucifer and all his fellows, and their bodies to the gallows of the Burrow Muir, first to be hanged, then torn apart by dogs, swine, and other wild beasts, abominable to all the world. And their life gone from your sight, as might their souls go from the sight of God...

Maledictions drawn from biblical curse-traditions were grounded in the common religious beliefs of the people; they were thus generally feared by the populace. However, in this instance the intended victims had little belief in the church's power, and the curse thus became a great source of amusement to the lawless raiders. This amusement was no doubt buoyed by the negligible impact the curse seems to have had upon them.

This particular curse has a modern footnote, as in 2001 Carlisle city council commissioned a local young artist, named Gordon Young, who was descended from the Reivers, to carve three hundred and eighty-one words of Dunbar's one-thousand and sixty-nine word curse upon a granite boulder as a millennial art project. The resultant installation was housed in an underpass between Carlisle Castle and the Tullie House museum. However, soon after the boulder was put in place a series of disasters and misfortunes beset the city of Carlisle, including floods, fires, disease, murder, and tragic deaths, for which the locals blamed upon the curse stone.

As a result, in 2005 the local Liberal Democrat councillor, Jim Tootle, put a motion before the council to have the stone destroyed or removed from the city, which he said was in response to the many constituents who had written to him demanding the same. However, the Bishop of Carlisle, the Right Reverend Dow, instead suggested the Archbishop of Glasgow, Mario Conti, should be called in to lift the curse.

The service of excommunication is also found in 'The Festival' (last printed in 1532). The 'General Sentence or Curse' contained in this old prayer book was intended to be said four times a year, and was regularly read by the presiding Abbot at Netley Abbey (Hampshire). First, each of the subjects of the Anathema was read out by name in English. Then the Bishop, being clothed in white, stood in the pulpit before the other priests of the church, and with uplifted cross and candles burning he delivered the thunderous curse in Latin, which translates as:

> By the authority of God the Father Almighty, and of the Blessed Virgin Mary, and all of the saints, we excommunicate, anathematise, and deliver over to the devil all the aforesaid malefactors; that excommunicated, anathematised, and delivered over to the devil they may be. Accursed be they in towns, in fields, in highways, in footpaths, under roof, out of doors, and in all other places, standing, lying, sitting down, rising up, walking, running, awake, asleep, eating, drinking, and doing whatsoever thing. From the illumination and all other good things of the church, we debar them. To the devil we condemn them. And in the pains of hell-fire we extinguish their souls—(unless they repent and make satisfaction)—even as this candle is extinguished.

The Bishop then rang his bell and extinguished the candle.

In John Adam's *Guide to Netley Abbey and the Neighbourhood* (1883), the Abbot's curse is linked to a mysterious death occurring at Netley Abbey. After the Dissolution of Netley in 1536, the 13th Century Cistercian abbey was converted into a fashionable Tudor house, but in 1704 the owner sold it for building materials. In 1719, a local builder named Walter Taylor was contracted to demolish the 13th Century church, and in return was granted the rights to use the abbey stone to erect a town house at Newport. However, before the work started, Taylor dreamt of being visited by a monk, who warned he would be punished for this sacrilege. In yet another dream Taylor saw himself being killed by a falling stone as he pulled down one of the church windows. Perplexed by these visions, Taylor sought the advice of a friend, who advised him the safest course of action would be to abandon his plan to level the holy edifice. However, despite the oneiric counsel, and the advice of his friend, Taylor decided to press ahead with the demolition of the church, but he had not got very far when the arch of a window fell upon his head and fractured his skull. Whilst it was initially thought the wound would not prove mortal, it was made worse by the butchery of an unskilled surgeon, and resulted in Taylor's life being brought to an abrupt end.

This story reflects the belief that curses would befall those committing acts of sacrilege, even without the intervention of God's ministers. In the Isle of Man, for example, a farmer from the parish of Jurby, who drove his sheep into an ancient church to shelter from a violent thunderstorm, realised his blasphemy when the following Spring he lost all his newborn lambs, many of which were born monstrosities. Also, when a farmer started dismantling a keeill (ancient chapel) on Camlork farm, he was suddenly struck with a great pain in his arm and had to stop work for some days. Undeterred, he later endeavoured to continue the task with the assistance of his wife and daughter, who both died soon after. This tragedy drove the man insane, and he remained in this state until his death.

Another case from the Isle of Man concerns a small windmill, which was erected using stones from an adjacent keeill for the purposes of driving a threshing machine. The moment the windmill was set to work it went with such fury that it shook the entire edifice, for which reason it was dismantled. Shortly thereafter, the owner of the farm on whose land the windmill was erected lost four cows and three horses to disease, which misfortune was attributed to the improper use of stones from a holy edifice. Other times the reuse of church stones not only brought misfortune, but also caused the buildings erected from them to be plagued by strange noises and poltergeist-like phenomena.

The curse invoked by the sacrilegious use of holy stones was so feared that its spectre was sometimes evoked in spoken maledictions. Indeed, the Manx ecclesiastic Bishop Wilson claimed many believed there to be no greater curse to a family than the words, *Clogh ny killagh ayns corneil dty hie mooar,* meaning "May a stone of the church be found in the corner of thy dwelling-house."[17] Implicit is the idea an enemy could be cursed by hiding an accursed stone in their house or land.

A particularly interesting case involving excommunication concerns the charges made against Dame Alice Kyteler in 1324. These included the accusation that, as a witch, she and her *sortilegae* held secret nocturnal conventicles where they impiously used the ceremonies of the church by lighting wax candles and pronouncing the rite of excommunication over people, including their own husbands.

This accursed rite was carried out by holding a lit candle and naming each part of the victim's body, 'from the soles of his or her feet to the top of the head.' Afterwards, the gathered assembly blew out the candles and exclaimed "fi, fi, fi, amen!"—*fi* is probably short for *fiat*, meaning 'let it be done'. There was also spitting at various points, 'as their ritual required.'

Whilst the practice of throwing lit tapers to the floor and stamping out the flame features in the rite of excommunication, the naming of parts of the victim from foot to crown is not. However, it is a common feature of those rites wherein witches gave themselves over to the Devil.[18] It could therefore be postulated that Kyteler's coven were working to excommunicate the named parties from the bosom of the church so that they might instead dedicate them to the Devil, thereby bringing them into their witchen fold.

Alternatively, the practice may relate to a passage from *Deuteronomy*

17 Moore, *The Folklore of the Isle of Man*, pp. 153–4.

18 Maxwell-Stuart, *The British Witch*, p. 46.

28, where it speaks of cursing an individual from the soles of their feet to the crown of their head, especially as *Deuteronomy* 28 was a favoured source of inspiration for maledictions and excommunications. Essentially, the assembled *sortilegae* may have been expressing their desire to curse the individual from head to foot. By naming each bodily part from head to foot whilst holding the candle, the taper became magically identified with the victim, and through this deed the witches procured a proxy for their curse. This is to say, the top, middle and bottom of the candle became as one with the victim's head, heart, and foot.

Whilst excommunications were generally pronounced by word and deed, they could also be written into a contract, which suggests the rite's power was retained even in written form. Commensurate are medieval book curses, which threatened excommunication on those who stole or damaged books, or who borrowed books but were slow to return them. As a great amount of work went into producing books in the medieval period, thus rendering them valuable commodities, it is unsurprising curses were invoked upon those stealing or defiling them. Implicit is the belief that written curses were tantamount to their performative equivalent, and as they were exacted by a preternatural force (God) rather than a human agency (the clergy), the book thief or vandal was subject to the curse whether or not they were found out during their lifetime.

A number of medieval book curses are collected in Marc Drogin's work, *Anathema! Medieval Scribes and the History of Book Curses* (1983). Some of the extant exemplars are simple in nature, cursing the victim with anathema only:

> May the sword of anathema slay
> If anyone steals this book away.

Simple curses were sometimes elaborated by threatening 'anathema-maranatha', thereby evoking *1 Corinthians* 16:22. Other times book curses were embellished with descriptions of the torment the curse would unleash:

> If anyone take away this book, let him die the death; let him be fried in a pan; let the falling sickness and fever size him; let him be broken on the wheel, and hanged. Amen.

And:

> For him that stealeth, or borroweth and returneth not, this book from its owner, let it change into a serpent in his hand and rend him. Let him be struck with palsy and all his members blasted. Let him languish in pain crying aloud for mercy, and let there be no surcease to his agony till he sing in dissolution. Let bookworms gnaw his entrails in token of the Worm that dieth not, and when at last he goeth to his final punishment, let the flames of Hell consume him for ever.

Comparable in nature are the curses included upon the edifice of the new library built on the instruction of Pope Sixtus V in the 1580s. Its entrance was flanked with large inscriptions detailing the dreadful maledictions that would befall those violating the library's regulations.[19]

Commensurate to book curses are the 'curse clauses' written into charters to protect property gifted to and owned by the church, which threatened imprecations against any who attempted to violate the church's rights. Illustrative is this 'curse clause' from a 12th Cen-

19 Little, 'The Separation of Religious Curses from Blessings in the Latin West', pp. 29–40.

tury charter, which documents the gifting of land to the church by a layperson:

> And if any wish to destroy this charter...may they have the curses of the three patriarchs, Abraham, Isaac, and Jacob; and of the four evangelists, Mark and Matthew, Luke and John; and of the twelve apostles and of the sixteen prophets and of the twenty-four elders and of the 318 holy fathers who deliberated on the canons at Nicea; and may they have the curse of the 144,000 martyrs who died for the Lord; and may they have the curse of the cherubim and the seraphim, who hold the throne of God, and of all the saints of God.[20]

Curse clauses were also written into wills, as demonstrated by this Anglo-Saxon Christian curse, which appears in the Will of Wulfguth dating from 1064. Not only does it curse the wrongdoer in this life, but also in that beyond:

> And he who shall detract from my will, which I have now declared in the witness of God, may be deprived of joy on this earth, and almighty God who created and made all creatures exclude him from the fellowship of all Saints on the day of Judgement and may he be delivered into the abyss of hell to Satan the devil and all his accursed companions and there with God's adversaries without end and never trouble my heirs.

Clerical Curses and the Reformation

BEtween the 11th and 13th Centuries, religious maledictions were called into question by evangelical reformers. They sought to curb the use of liturgical curses, arguing the making of clamours and maledictions betrayed a lack of faith in God and His ability to exercise

20 Little, *Benedictine Maldeictions*, p. 56.

His own judgment and justice. During the same period a move was made across Europe to oust the custom of making specific curses as-and-when the need arose by instead providing a calendar of dates during which more generic curses against all sinners could be invoked. Typically, the ruling was for maledictions to be made three or four times a year on important feast days. In 1195, a synod held at York stipulated that:

> ...we do order that, for the future, every priest, three times in the year, with candles lighted and bells ringing, shall solemnly excommunicate those who, in recognizances and other matters of testimony, shall have knowingly and wilfully been guilty of perjury, and shall on every Lord's day denounce them as excommunicated, to the end that the frequent repetition of the malediction may withdraw those from their iniquity, whom the accusation of their own conscience does not deter therefrom.[21]

Yet, whilst the medieval church continued to maintain the power and right of its clergy to bestow curses, the calls for an end to such practices continued to grow, which protestations reached their head during the English Reformation. These Protestant reformers not only poured scorn on the idea of priestly curses, but argued that God did not require a human intermediary to act on His behalf; if His law had been broken, He would curse the transgressors Himself. They considered it blasphemous, and a challenge to God's omnipotence, for priests to claim the power to work such miracles, because in so doing they presumed an ability to command and manipulate the Almighty.

On this basis, the Anglican Church dropped the practices of liturgical maledictions, clamours, and excommunication. However, the Church of England did allow the reading of *Deuteronomy* 28 within its Service of Commination. The service of the 'Commination, or Denouncing of God's Anger and Judgements Against Sinners' was essentially the English Reformation's answer to the earlier tradition of liturgical maledictions. It enabled the clergy to recite a litany against the sinner(s), reminding them of the punishments God visited upon those

21 Ibid., 36.

transgressing His law. This threat of divine vengeance was essentially a stick by which to coerce sinners into changing their ways.

The rite itself was carried out before Communion, and involved the priest reciting a series of curses that would be meted out to sinners. After each one was read, the congregation would reply "Amen", i.e. 'so be it'. This rite, which was literally 'a threatening of vengeance', was published in the first edition of the *Book of Common Prayer* (1549) as part of the Ash Wednesday observances, although later editions advised it could be used on other occasions also. The justification for this service was that it carried on the 'godly discipline' established by the early church of putting to public penance those who stood convicted of notorious sin, which penance was traditionally carried out at the beginning of Lent.

This Protestant rite was theoretically a general petition to God to curse all impenitent sinners, rather than a malediction aimed at a specific offender. However, in practice this was not always the case.[22] Indeed, even as late as 1963, the 72-year-old Anglican vicar of St. Nicholas (Bramber, Sussex), Ernest Streete, pronounced the Rite of Commination as a specific curse against some unknown 'black magicians', which group had defiled his church by daubing its flagstones with 'magical signs' and disinterring gravestones and a stone cross. During the Sunday service he asked the congregation to rise and then invoked the Service of Commination, afterwards declaring:

> I pronounce a curse on those who touched God's acre in this churchyard...and for their sacrilege and the terrible thoughts in their minds. I will not relent until they apologise or ask for forgiveness. May their days be of anguish and sorrow, and may God have mercy on their souls.

Although the use of counter-curses has a long history in the church, many parishioners and local clergymen were displeased with what they thought of as 'a return to medieval superstition'. Indeed, a spokesman for the Church of England said the rector had no right to invoke such a thunderous curse without first seeking the Bishop's permission. Howev-

22 Keith Thomas, *Religion and the Decline of Magic*, p. 601.

er, the rector was unrepentant, and had in fact delivered a similar curse 20 years previous when a thief had stolen from the church's moneybox, which malediction led to the money's successful and swift return.[23]

When the Revd. Streete walked to his church the following Monday morning, the damaged gravestones and cross had been repaired and returned to their proper places, and the occult daubing had been removed. Believing his curse to have been successful, he formally revoked it, declaring:

> My curse has worked...they have repented. All it needed was a firm hand. I shall withdraw the curse.

However, this time it was not the curse that had righted the wrong, but rather the local constabulary, who had kindly repaired the damage on the Sunday evening.[24]

Despite the objections of reformers, some argued in support of the Roman Catholic Church's use of excommunication and anathema. Chief amongst these were the Jesuits, and in 1615 the German Jesuit, Jacob Gretser, published a tract on the subject of benedictions and maledictions, wherein he defended the priestly use of curses by referencing the many biblical curses made by God, Jesus, and the prophets. He also referred to the justification advanced by Gregory the Great, who contended curses made by holy personages were not made out of a desire for revenge but rather a desire for justice to be served.[25]

However, even though holy maledictions were prohibited Post-Reformation, the practice did not entirely die out, and was often continued in places where Catholicism had a stronghold. For example, when some church silver was purloined in 1628, the Bishop of Barcelona put a curse on the land surrounding the site of the theft, which caused any crops planted there to become ruined.[26]

During the Reformation, Henry VIII set about disbanding the many English and Irish monasteries, priories, convents, and friaries, which

23 *The Register Guard*, 26th January 1964.

24 Tom A Cullen, 'When Black Magic is Afoot, the Aged Rector Simply Has to Curse'. *Desert Sun*, Number 133, 7th January, 1964.

25 Little, 'The Separation of Religious Curses from Blessings in the Latin West', p. 37.

26 Thomas, p. 600.

event became known as the Dissolution of the Monasteries. In doing so, he appropriated their great wealth and disposed of their many assets, which were used to fund the activities of the Crown. Folklore suggests the affected monks sometimes retaliated by making maledictions, which is attested by the array of tales concerning monks placing curses on those who aided in the Dissolution, or who received the lands and goods confiscated from them during the Reformation. Moreover, because 'ill-gotten gains never prosper', it was believed the monks' curses would be passed down the victim's family line, becoming generational curses causing their descendants financial ruin, death, and misfortune. Examples of this narrative are found in numerous books and pamphlets from the 17th century onwards, including Henry Spelman's *The History and Fate of Sacrilege* (1698).[27]

One example of a monk's generational curse is that associated with the House of Cowdray (Sussex). During the 16th Century, King Henry VIII gifted Battle Abbey to Sir Anthony Browne as a reward for his help in closing down the monasteries. Whilst Browne celebrated the Abbey's successful conversion into a private residence, a monk pronounced a curse upon him and his descendants, declaring they would die 'by fire and water'. The monk's curse seemingly met with success; not only did great misfortune plague Browne's descendants, but in 1793 the last of the line drowned, and a great fire destroyed the family home (Cowdray Place), thereby fulfilling the prophecy of destruction 'by fire and water.'

Another tale concerns a medieval well between the borders of Rainhill and Sutton St. Helens, which was dedicated to St. Anne. According to a local legend, St. Anne bathed in this well pool, which sanctified the waters and gave them a restorative power. As a result, pilgrims flocked to the well, and until the 19th Century its waters were much sought after for the healing of eye and skin diseases. The well-pool was about 4-feet deep and accessed by steps leading into it, thereby enabling pilgrims to submerge themselves in its waters.

To help manage the great number of visiting pilgrims, several buildings were erected around the well, and it was placed into the custodianship of two monks from a nearby priory. According to a report in the *St. Helen's Leader* from 1877, there was a dispute in the 16th Century

27 Simpson and Roud, *The Oxford Dictionary of English Folklore.*

when the estate manager of the neighbouring land, Hugh Darcy, became frustrated with the amount of space the well was taking up. These simmering tensions came to a head during a standoff at the well, when Darcy told the prior, Father Delwaney, that he didn't think he would be in the position for much longer. Sure enough, just two days later the king's commissioners arrived and took possession of both the priory and the well.

Father Delwaney blamed Darcy for this turn of events, and, seething with anger, pronounced a curse on him. He declared that Darcy would be dead within a year and a day, and then, with his words still ringing in the air, Dalwaney collapsed and died. Soon after the prior's dramatic death the curse began to take effect. First, Darcy's son died of a mysterious illness, and then Darcy himself suffered huge financial losses, which drove him to drink, and then after a heavy night in a tavern, he disappeared. A search was instigated, and Darcy's lifeless body was later found beside the well, his head having been crushed in. How Darcy met this grisly fate was never discovered, but locals believed it a fulfilment of the prior's curse.

A tale of cursing monks is also preserved in a Croatian legend from Lokrum, a small island off Dubrovnik. Their curse was incepted when a General of the French army ordered the closure of the island's Benedictine monastery and the expulsion of all its monks. When the monks' efforts to remain in the monastery failed, they went by night to the island's church, which was dedicated to St. Mary, to carry out one final Mass. As they left the church, they donned their hooded robes and carried lit tapers in a solemn procession about the island. These candles were symbolically turned upside down, causing the wax to fall upon the earth, and as they processed they chanted, "Whosoever claims Lokrum for his own personal pleasure shall be damned!" By the foot planted upon the earth, and the droplets of consecrated wax fallen to earth, the land was seeded with their imprecatory prayer, and by processing about the islands' bounds, they placed the enclosed plot under the influence of their malefic spell.

The monks processed three times about the island, which took all night, and when dawn broke, they took to their boat and sailed away without looking back. According to legend, this curse resulted in several members of the island's aristocratic families meeting untimely and violent ends, and for several centuries after every new owner of the island was plagued with misfortune.

Whilst the Protestant church denounced the idea curses could be invoked in God's name, they maintained the belief that God cursed those who worked against Him, as demonstrated by numerous salutary tales preserved in Protestant works. Illustrative is an incident occurring during the reign of Henry VII, when a papist chancellor named Dr. Whittington burnt a protestant woman for heresy, which woman was described by protestant sympathisers as, 'a faithful woman and true servant of God.' After the Catholic executioners had finished their work, a bull due for the slaughter escaped its restraints and gored the chancellor to death, dragging his innards through the streets, much to the delight of the onlookers. Protestants interpreted this as being the work of God, thereby proving (in their minds at least) that God was on their side.

A comparable tale is related in John Foxe's 16th Century work, *Actes and Monuments* (also known as *Foxe's Book of Martyrs*). It tells how William Grimwood of Hitcham was struck down by God for perjuring himself against John Cooper at the Bury St Edmund Assizes—'suddenly his bowels fell out of his body, and immediately most miserably he died: such was the terrible judgement of God.' This divine punishment is somewhat reminiscent of the death of Judas the betrayer in *Acts* 1:18, '...and falling headlong, he burst asunder in the middle, and all his bowels gushed out.'

These cautionary tales, which confirm God's penchant for retribution against His enemies, were employed by church and state to keep people in line. This is to say they used the idea of a vengeful God to frighten, and thereby coerce, the populace into doing things the church and state deemed as being 'God's will', and into conforming to behaviours the authorities declared as 'Christian'. Herein is demonstrated the way a state's official and dominant religion was, and still is, used as a carrot and stick to goad and jade its peoples towards its own ends.

Biblical verses were also pressed into service for the purposes of coercing the populace into conforming to the will of the authorities. Illustrative is the use of *Judges* 5:23, 'Curse ye Meroz, said the angel of the Lord, curse you bitterly and the inhabitants thereof; because they came not to the help of the Lord against the mighty.' This verse, wherein an angel pronounces a curse upon a place and its people for refusing to fight God's enemies, has been used throughout history as a means of motivating, cajoling, and threatening those reticent to join wars and endeavours the church deemed righteous. Indeed, it was extensively used for this purpose by preachers during the 17th Century English Civil War and the 18th Century American Revolution. Another biblical passage enlisted for such purposes was *Jeremiah* 48:10, 'cursed be he that keepeth back his sword from blood.'

Predictably, whilst the making of maledictions was officially prohibited, the clergy frequently flouted church policy, and this included many Protestant clerics. For example, in 1618 one Puritan minister hurled curses from the pulpit at parishioners who walked out of his lengthy sermons, and in the 1640s the Puritan clergyman, Thomas Larkham, was accused of pronouncing the 'curse of God' upon a parishioner in Tavistock. Many other tales illustrating the clergy's proclivity for invoking thunderous curses are peppered throughout the church's history, from its very earliest days into the modern period, which considering the nature of the human condition is perhaps unsurprising.

The continuing use of priestly curses was particularly evident in Ireland, and was frequently used by Roman Catholic clergymen to smite sinners, Protestant missionaries, and Unionists. Irish priests also uttered their curses in the Irish neighbourhoods of mainland Britain. For example, in the 1850s there were reports that Irish priests were using the threat of malediction to deter Catholic parents from enrolling their children in National Schools run by Protestants in London, and in some cases the priests even took to the pulpits to curse those who had defied them. On a mundane level, this served to cut the individual off from their community. As one Londoner said, "If he [the priest] curses me, no man or woman is allowed to speak to me." Yet, aside from social ostracisation, the priest's curse could sometimes obtain more magical effect. Indeed, one cursed family were transfixed to the spot, as if nailed to the floor, until the priest absolved them.[28] Notably, transfixion was also a common result of certain witch curses.

Whilst rarer, modern cases of cursing by British clergyman are not unknown. One such example concerns the Revd. Carter Moore, who was the son of a clergyman, and a graduate of St. John's College (Cambridge). Whilst serving as a curate of Flordon (Norfolk), the Reverend's fractious and argumentative nature riled many parishioners, and in 1852 the village postman roughed him up. Whilst the Reverend wanted to prosecute, the local magistrate instead wrote to the priest's father and suggested his trouble-making son should leave the village. This only served to further anger Revd. Carter-Moore, who being denied legal aid, sought revenge on the magistrate. On Sunday 13th March 1852, the Reverend was waiting on the platform of Flordon train station for the 5 o'clock train in full clerical vestments. When the train came in, the magistrate, William Gwyn JP, stepped off, and when the reverend saw him he began to pronounce his curse, "I curse you; I curse your wife; I curse your children; I curse all you have; may your children be fatherless and vagabonds, and beg their bread." The curate's curse was overheard by the other travellers, and the story was subsequently reported in the national press. The magistrate was terrified for his life, and whilst the reverend was thereafter arrested, and subsequently removed from his position by the Bishop of Norwich, he continued his religious career by working as a chaplain and curate in other parishes.[29]

Further illustrative of the modern belief in the clerical curse is the malediction allegedly placed on the 1951 Mayo (Ireland) football team.

28 Thomas Waters, *Cursed Britain*, p. 45.

29 Ibid., 47–8.

After a win against Meath, the team jubilantly headed home from Dublin, passing a funeral in the town of Foxford on their way. The team's failure to stop and show respect outraged the officiating priest (or in some versions, holy woman), which prompted the minister to pronounce a curse upon them, declaring that Mayo would never win the All-Ireland championship until all members of the 1951 team had died. This curse resulted in a run of ill-luck, with the team losing every championship thereafter. Although surviving members of the team have denied the story, and there are no references in the parish records to corroborate the curse, in 2016 the Foxford Catholic priest, Father Costello officially blessed the Mayo senior footballers in an attempt to nullify the curse.

Magical Maledictions and the Black Mass

WHilst the Church has demonstrated a rather ambivalent attitude towards clergy pronouncing maledictions invoking God's judgment, it has always been clear in its condemnation of curses employing more 'magical' elements. For example, in 694 the Seventeenth Council of Toledo officially forbade priests from saying funeral masses for the living, which was done as a death-curse, and like other illicit maledictions was an inversion of an approved service:

> Some priests hold Masses for the dead, on behalf of the living, that these may soon die. The priest who does this, and the person who induced him to do it, shall both be deposed and forever anathematised and excommunicated. Only on their deathbed may the communion be again administered to them.

These masses, wherein the priest wears the traditional black vestments of the Latin Mass for the Dead (or Requiem Mass), were known as 'black masses'. By saying the Requiem Mass in the name of a living victim, the priest hoped to cause the named party an early death. However, as the priest could say the victim's name(s) mentally, any attempted *ma-*

leficia would be difficult to ascertain, and in most cases the congregation would remain ignorant of the priest's true intentions.

A comparable practice, which was prohibited by the Council of Trier in 1227, was the displaying of biers in churches whilst celebrating Requiem Masses for the living, 'so that they die sooner.' During Christian burials the bier was often placed in the centre of the nave, with lit candles about it, and remained there for the duration of the funeral. The display of the bier in the illicit rite was thus intended to represent the bier on which the minister desired the victim's corpse to soon lay, and was essentially an act of sympathetic magic.

A more elaborate example of a Requiem Mass said to hasten the demise of a living victim is recounted in the 15th Century treatise *Dives and Pauper*, which condemns those who:

> ...for the hate or wrath that they bear against any man or woman take away the clothes of the altar, and clothe the altar with doleful clothing, or beset the altar or the cross about with thorns, and withdraw light out of the church or...do sing mass of requiem for them that be alive, in hope that they should fare the worse and the sooner die.

Whilst these forbidden practices were sometimes carried out by laypeople, it is clear the clergy themselves were frequently involved.[30] For example, in 17th Century France, the notorious sorcerer and fortuneteller, Catherine Monvoisin (known as La Voisin), was renowned for arranging black masses on behalf of clients, which were worked for various magical ends, including wish-fulfilment, love, lust, and the bringing of death and misfortune upon enemies. These black masses were officiated by priests known to La Voisin, including François Mariotte and Etienne Guiborg, which pair carried out the black masses in the infamous Affair of the Poisons.

A more involved illicit rite was the Mass of St. Sécaire, which could be said for vengeance upon troublesome neighbours, unscrupulous moneylenders, recalcitrant lovers, and enemies. Saint Sécaire is likely commensurate with Saint Sequayre, whom the Basques prayed to that

30 Thomas, pp. 37–8.

their enemies might slowly wither away and die. The Mass of St. Sécaire was to be held in a church that had been abandoned, defiled, or fallen into disrepair, and the priest was to be attended by a female accomplice with whom he had engaged in carnal deeds. The Mass was to be recited backwards, starting at eleven o'clock and finishing at the stroke of midnight, and whenever the Mass called for the sign of the cross to be made, the priest was to draw it on the ground with his left foot. Also, the white circular host was to be replaced with a black triangular host, and the consecrated wine was to be replaced with water from a well in which an unbaptised infant had been drowned. At the end of the rite, the priest announced the name of the victim against whom the Mass was said, and this would cause the named party to waste away and die. Laypersons are alleged to have paid renegade priests substantial sums to carry out variations of St. Seçaire's Mass in Gascony and other parts of France, and the rite was still greatly feared in the 19th Century.[31]

St. Seçaire's was not the only unorthodox Mass practiced in France. Other examples include the *messe de male-mort*, which was said in Bigorre for usurers and inconstant lovers, and the *messe sèche*, which was said in Saint Saud to cause a sharecropper, who had turned a beggar away, to suffer a long illness from which he eventually died.

Masses to cause the injury and death of one's relatives and enemies were still practiced as late as the 20th Century, and in an attempt to stamp out this custom, priests took to the pulpit to deliver sermons condemning the practice. The masses themselves were carried out by laypeople and clerics alike. For example, in 1500, the bishop of Cambrai complained to the University of Paris that his deans and canons were cursing him by inserting condemnatory passages from the Old Testament into the Mass, which were being read by the priest with his back to the altar, and with the choir singing in response; his complaint was upheld.

Some priests charged considerable sums of money to say wish-fulfilling masses on behalf of others. In Normandy, for example, laypeople

31 Devlin, Judith, *The Superstitious Mind: French Peasants and the Supernatural in the Nineteenth Century*, pp. 18–20. A graphic description of the rite in English is found in James Frazer's *Golden Bough* (1890), and is based on the description in Jean-François Bladé's *Quatorze Superstitions Populaires de la Gascogne* (*Fourteen Popular Superstitions of Gascony*, 1883).

paid priests to say the *messe du Saint Esprit* to force God to grant their desires. Priests also took a fee to say the Votive Mass on behalf of laypeople to procure their desired boon, whether protection, love, health, the laying of spirits, or cursing of enemies. For example, a Canadian Oblate priest working in the mining district of Northern Potosi (Bolivia) was once approached by a peasant who asked him to say a Mass for a severed head, which was causing him and his family trouble.[32]

Another Canadian Oblate priest working in Bolivia, named Jacques Monast, was asked on occasion to say a 'cursing mass' (*misa de maldiction*).[33] This cursing mass was intended to invoke God's judgment upon the petitioner's enemy so as to procure divine justice, and was usually worked to punish thieves, fraudsters, trespassers, slanderers, and adulterers. However, some requested the Mass in cases of jealousy, and also in disputes regarding land ownership and inheritance.

Many believed the curse mass would only punish the truly guilty, and if falsely brought to bear would backfire upon the one requesting it. Illustrative is a case concerning a cleric from Boulieu (France), who was asked by a peasant to say a cursing mass to cause the death of his neighbour, with whom he was in litigation. Whilst the peasant believed himself to be in the right, the priest warned him God would be the ultimate judge, and knowing who was right would kill the true guilty party. In consideration of this, the peasant withdrew his request that he might talk it over with his wife.[34]

Curses were also effected by saying certain masses over effigies. For example, in Chapter 49 of *Gemma Ecclesiastica* ('Jewel of the Church'), the archdeacon Giraldus Cambrensis (Gerald of Wales, 1146–1223) relates how the mass for the dead was said over wax poppets:

> Again, I say it with tears, that some have abused this great sacrament for purposes of magic by celebrating masses over waxen images to bring down curses on others. Sometimes in this spirit of imprecation the '*Missa Fidelium*' has been sung over a man ten times or more, that he might

32 Fennella Cannell, (ed), *The Anthropology of Christianity*, p. 74.

33 Ibid., 74.

34 Judith Devlin, *The Superstitious Mind*, pp. 18–20.

> die within ten days after, and be buried 'among the dead.'

These wax poppets were presumably buried after the Requiem Mass to complete the analogical act of magic. Gerald gleaned his knowledge of this practice from a 12th Century work by the French Catholic theologian, Peter the Chanter, from whom he copied the information word for word.[35]

Poppets made for the purposes of magical manipulation were often baptised, which sacrament established a connection between the effigy and the victim, even as baptism conferred a name upon the newborn. This misuse of a Christian rite for magical purposes is comparable to the abuse of holy water and consecrated hosts, and was much condemned by the church during the 13th and 14th centuries.[36]

Illustrating the baptism of poppets is a case from 1315 concerning the Bishop of Cahors (Hugues Géraud) and his ecclesiastical accomplices, who made several attempts on the life of Pope John XXII and two cardinals using wax dolls. On one occasion the wax dolls were cast from a mould by a 'baptised Jew' named Bernard Jourdain, and then blessed in a church ceremony, but were intercepted before they could reach the bishop. On another occasion Géraud obtained a wax figure from Toulouse and was taught by a local Jew how to use it. This involved baptising the effigy, reciting certain words over it, and then pricking it in certain places at certain times. They wrote 'may [name] die' on each one, and then baptised the effigies in full ritual form in order to secure the death of the named victims through sorcery, as this account explains:

> [Géraud] baptised it, sprinkling holy water on it and anointing it with chrism, reciting prayers and words written in a book he was holding. Afterwards, according to the instructions of the Jew, the aforementioned bishop [Géraud] pierced it in the stomach with a stylus, and the witness [Pierre Fouquier] pierced it in the side with a needle, saying "*May those who persecute me be thwarted,*"

35 Priscilla Heath Barnum, *Dives and Pauper Volume 2*, 2004, p. 67.

36 Kati Ihnat and Katelyn Mesler, 'From Christian Devotion to Jewish Sorcery: The Curious History of Wax Figurines in Medieval Europe'.

> etc. (Jer. 17:18), "*May his days be few,*" (Ps. 108:8), and the remaining verses of that Psalm. Having done this, they placed the aforementioned image as though it were dead on its back, in a chest of the aforementioned bishop.[37]

It was alleged the bishop and his malefactors had previously used this magical technique to assassinate the Pope's favourite nephew, Cardinal Jacques de Via.

Another example concerns Bishop Guichard de Troyes, who in 1308 was charged with using a wax doll to kill Queen Jeanne in 1305, and of employing the services of a sorceress and a Dominican friar skilled in necromancy to aid in the work. To determine the best way to proceed the friar conjured a demon, and after the bishop paid the spirit homage, the mortal trio were told to make a wax image resembling the Queen, baptise it in her name, and prick it in the head and neck with a needle, which would cause her to become ill. However, should they wish her to die they were to instead melt the doll in a fire. Taking the demon's advice, Guichard made a wax doll, and the three malefactors went in disguise to the Sainte-Flavy hermitage, where the bishop and friar baptised the graven image in the name of Queen Jeanne, and set about piercing various parts of its body. The Queen subsequently fell ill, and her physicians were unable to restore her to health. However, although the bishop goaded the sorceress to repeatedly stab the wax doll, the Queen would not die. Frustrated, the bishop broke the image asunder, trampled it, and cast it into a fire, which caused the Queen's immediate death.

A further example demonstrating the medieval association of image magic with baptism concerns the death of the bishop Eberhard, who met his end in the sanctuary on Holy Saturday in 1066. According to information added to the *Deeds of the Treveri* (a chronicle of Trier) circa 1132, Eberhard's death was the result of magical retribution for his decree that all Jews were to be expelled from the city, unless they converted by Holy Saturday:

37 Rome, ASV, Collection 493, fol. 21r (deposition of Pierre Fouquier, 6th July 1317).

> And so, certain ones of that wicked race [the Jews], after fashioning a wax image (*imaginem*) in likeness of the bishop, which they placed among the candles (*lichnis*), bribed a certain cleric of the monastery of Saint Paul, a Christian in name but not in deed, to baptise it. On that Saturday, after the bishop had already prepared for the solemn celebrations of baptism, they lit it on fire. Once half of it had burned, the bishop, who was presiding over the holy offices at the [baptismal] font...fell gravely ill and...died.

In addition to baptism, masses were also said over poppets to empower them and endow them with a spiritual strength that could be used against the victim.[38] For example, in 1441 the Duchess of Gloucester was accused of conspiring to magically end the life of King Henry VI, who was just nineteen years old at the time, by means of a wax doll to help her husband gain the throne. Having no magical experience, the Duchess enlisted the help of Canon Thomas Southwell, a priest named Roger Bolingbroke, and a wise woman named Margery Jourdemayne, who was colloquially known as 'the Witch of Eye' (on account of the fact she hailed from the Manor of Eye-next-Westminster). The wax doll and materials used in this magical operation were empowered when Canon Thomas Southwell secretly said the Mass over them in Hornsey Park. Despite the Duchess's protestations that the doll was a fertility charm made to help her gain a brood of her own, the prosecution won out. The Duchess was sentenced to public penance followed by life imprisonment, Canon Southwell died in prison, Margery was burnt at the stake in Smithfield, and Bolingbroke was hung, drawn and quartered, with his severed head being displayed on London Bridge and his four limbs being displayed at York, Oxford, Cambridge, and Hereford.[39]

Another instance demonstrating the use of the Mass to empower poppets concerns an organised magical attempt on the life of Henry III of France in 1589, although this rite did not succeed in attaining its desired outcome. In a diary entry dated 26th January, Pierre de l'Estoile

38 Christina Hole, *Witchcraft in England*, p. 120.

39 Ibid., 118–121.

recorded how the disaffected citizens of Paris used wax images to try and rid themselves of him:

> ...images of wax [portraying Henry III] were kept on altars and were pierced during forty masses given during forty hours in Paris, and the fortieth they pierced the image at the spot where the heart would be, saying at each piercing some magic word in their efforts to bring death to the king.

In order to avoid prosecution, those desiring to have their poppets magically vivified by power of the Mass would sometimes surreptitiously conceal them beneath the altar. For example, it is written in the *Malleus Maleficarum* how wax images and aromatic substances were sometimes empowered by being placed under the altar cloth, after which they were hidden beneath the threshold of a house so as to bewitch those crossing over it. Of course, the poppets empowered by virtue of their sojourn beneath the altar could be used for other purposes. For example, in Venice a woman placed 'a wax statue punctured with needles under the altar in the local church' to force her husband to return to her.[40]

In the 14th Century *Hygromanteia* (or The Magical Treatise of Solomon), it is similarly written how poppets should be made from beeswax that has spent three days in a church, and has thus been present for the saying of a Mass. After the operant has called upon the holy names of the Angel Adonai, this wax is then modelled into the desired form. In 1613, the Reformed minister, Anton Praetorius related how wax figures were believed to be made efficacious when wrought by a monk or priest, which effigy was thereafter consecrated by the ecclesiast saying Mass over it for three Sundays.

Another type of malefic magic associated with priests was the *noument de l'aiguillette* ('knotting of the cord'), which ligature spell was used to cause impotence. It was worked by knotting a cord during the marriage ceremony, and in 1632 a frustrated married couple accused a clergyman from Azay-le-Brûlé of 'tying the knot' against them. In 1650 another priest was not only charged with working this ligature spell,

40 Bever, *The Realities of Witchcraft and Popular Magic in Early Modern Europe*, p 154.

but also of seeking to extort a fee from the bewitched couple in exchange for undoing it.[41]

Such illicit magical practices led many to mistrust the clergy, and to consider them as powerful sorcerers who were just as likely to curse an individual as bless them.[42] For example, in 1672 locals accused a vicar on the Isle of Man of killing some sheep by casting the evil eye on them, much in the manner of a witch.[43] Some of God's ministers were even accused of being in league with witches, and in 1517 the Council of Florence decreed heavy penalties to be levied on members of the clergy caught selling Eucharistic materials to witches.

Also unorthodox in nature were the curses issued by the many 'false prophets' who once preached throughout Britain. For example, in London 1936, two weavers named Richard Farnham and John Bull claimed to be divine prophets with the power to inflict plagues upon mankind and to know of things to come. Farnham also claimed to be one of the two witnesses spoken of in *Revelation* 11, and he declared 'the Lord hath given me power for the opening and shutting of the heavens.' For this imposture the High Commission imprisoned the two men, and they died in 1642, although both claimed they would rise again.

In the 1650s another pair claimed to be the Two Witnesses of Revelation, which pair consisted of two tailors named John Reeve and Lodowick Muggleton. Muggleton was particularly fond of pronouncing ceremonial curses, which he issued both in person and by letter, and several of his victims died soon thereafter. On one occasion Muggleton cursed the English Ranter, John Robins (himself no stranger to cursing), for deceiving people with his claims of having divine power. As a result, Robins was immediately stricken with a sudden 'burning in his throat.' On another occasion Muggleton's victim was first struck dumb, then fell sick, and finally fell down dead, just ten days after the curse had been pronounced.[44]

Another 'false prophet' with a reputation for cursing was the early 17th Century Anabaptist and Arian, Edward Wightman, who claimed to be the Elijah foretold in *Malachi* 4:5. Like his biblical namesake, he

41 Owen Davies, *Grimoires*, pp. 72–3.

42 Devlin, *The Superstitious Mind*, pp. 18–20.

43 Maxwell-Stuart, *The British Witch*, p. 326.

44 Thomas, *Religion and the Decline of Magic*, pp. 159–60, 602, 609.

declared those who ridiculed his claims would be cursed and would meet the same fate as the children who mocked Elijah. Wightman was burnt for heresy in 1612, and was the last Englishman to be sent to the stake for this crime.[45]

45 Ibid., 159–60.

3

Grimoires, the Conjuring Clergy, and the Cunning Folk

A PARTICULARLY RICH source of magico-religious curses are the various texts constituting the grimoire tradition, which are replete with pseudo-Christian magic drawing upon orthodox liturgy, such as the use of prayer, Psalms, Latin conjurations, and exorcisms. These pseudo-Christian formulas are sometimes married with simpler acts of folk magic, for example the use of wax dolls and magical images, which methods frequently betray pagan influences.

A great number of grimoires proclaim to originate from the hands of biblical figures, after whom they are sometimes named, and include Enoch, Moses (the *Eighth Book of Moses*, *The Sword of Moses*, and *The Sixth and Seventh Book of Moses*), and King Solomon (*The Testament of Solomon* and *Clavicula Salomonis*). Some were also named after saints and ecclesiasts, such as the Grimoire of Pope Honorius, and the various Books of St. Cyprian of Antioch, which saint was reputedly a pagan sorcerer who converted to Christianity.

Other grimoires are credited with more otherworldly origins. One example is the *Smagorad*, which Arnaud Guillaume, a 14th century ascetic sorcerer from Guienne, claimed was a copy of a book an angel gave to Adam on God's command. This heaven-sent book gave power over the stars and planets, and was purportedly gifted to Adam that he might find consolation within its pages after having mourned Abel's death for a hundred years. It was anticipated that the knowledge within the *Smagorad* would help Adam recover all he had forfeited in sinning.

Some of these grimoires were handed (or copied) down through the generations, a deed which forged a great chain linking the book's owner to its originating author. Others were allegedly hidden by their authors for discovery at a later date, ensuring the book's secrets would be available for future generations.

Practitioners using grimoires authored by Moses, King Solomon, and other wise and pious Christian luminaries, contended the magic within was of Godly origin, and therefore licit. However, the Church disputed this, and remained resolute in its condemnation of pseudo-Christian magical texts. Nonetheless, grimoires remained popular with the priesthood, and during the medieval period were readily available in many European ecclesiastical universities, as attested by the 12th Century bishop of Paris, William of Auvergne, who recalled handling numerous books of magic during his studies. Prior to the Reformation, monastic libraries were amongst the largest depositories of occult works,[1] and until the 15th Century, the clergy pretty much had the monopoly on access to these texts. Those minor clergy, parish priests, monks, and curates who disseminated and used the texts were considered the 'clerical underworld' of magic.

The presence of occult texts in monastic and ecclesiastic libraries was justified by the need of clerics and monks to understand what magicians were doing, ostensibly for the purposes of condemning their activities. However, it is clear from the evidence many also sought instruction from these occult tomes that they might undertake a range of magico-religious activities, including natural magic, ritual magic, alchemy, and the making of astrological amulets. Of all ecclesiasts, monks and friars had perhaps the greatest opportunity to indulge in these magical arts; they not only had access to the books held in monastic libraries, and the ability to read and understand them, but also the free time needed to study the magical systems contained therein.

This proclivity for magic is illustrated in the reports made by bishops when visiting monasteries to uncover irregularities and abuses, which frequently contain references to monks practicing magic. For example, in 1440, the Augustinian abbot of Leicester, William Sadyngton, was accused of using the fingernail of a young boy to foretell the future,

1 Davies, *Grimoires*, p. 36.

which practice was ostensibly learnt from one of the many works on natural magic and divination known to have been held in Leicester Abbey's library. It is presumed religious specialists undertaking such activities had reconciled their own Christian faith with what many considered as 'devilish arts'.[2]

Ecclesiasts were uniquely placed in the deployment of ritual magic, not only by dint of their privileged access to grimoires and the many sacred substances necessary for the operations therein, but also because they possessed the level of education and literacy needed to understand the Latin texts and compose the written charms. In addition, the pseudo-Christian nature of the texts made a rudimentary knowledge of Church ritual and exorcism a prerequisite to properly employ them, as many operations relied upon the ability of the practitioner to subvert their mastery of this ritual art towards more illicit purposes.[3]

Ecclesiasts were further commended to the learned magical arts by the necessity to be 'clean' and 'godly' in order to control, and not be overcome or tempted by, the various spirits and demons conjured, which the clergy (in theory at least) were. To this end, before proceeding with any conjurations, the grimoires instruct the operant to undertake various purificatory and offeratory practices, which beseech God and His heavenly retinue to aid the work and make the magician strong. Illustrative is the *Grimoire of Pope Honorius*, wherein the Mass is a key element of the magical operations, and is intended to make the magician pure and godly, thereby allowing him or her to traffic with and control demons without succumbing.

In essence, the Christian magus sought to use God's power to conjure and command the demonic horde to satisfy their own (or their client's) desire. Implicit is the belief that God aided, and thus approved of, their work, and on this basis, they differentiated their magic from the practice of vulgar diabolism, despite the Church's protestations to the contrary. However, clerical magicians did not always work for charitable purposes, and many poorer ecclesiasts used their godly reputation and unique access to occult texts to work magic for personal financial gain.[4]

2 Francis Young, 'The Dissolution of the Monasteries and the Democratisation of Magic in Post-Reformation England'. *Religions*, Vol 10 Issue 4, 2019.

3 Davies, *Grimoires*, pp. 36–7.

4 Ibid., 63.

The use of grimoires by ecclesiasts was still common in the 16th Century, and after a number of witch trials in France involving the priesthood and their grimoires, the French judge Pierre de Lancre became preoccupied with the increasing problem of 'witch priests'. However, the number of ecclesiasts practicing ritual magic was much exaggerated during the Reformation. Indeed, accusations that monks and friars were practitioners of quasi-religious superstitions, and dabblers in the dark arts, was part of the Reformers agenda to blacken the reputation of Catholicism, and thereby further justify the dissolution of the abbeys.

After the Reformation, when dispossessed monks had to find new roles in society, many took up occupations putting their learnedness to use, which included the posts of parish clergy and schoolmaster. Others used their skill-set to set up as magical specialists. For example, in 1546 a former monk of Bury St. Edmunds, William Blomfild, was accused by his servant, John Morvill, of making a magic circle for the practice of necromancy and of using a book to control the weather. Another former monk, named John Coxe, was brought before a Kent magistrate in 1561 for saying 'a mass to call on the devil', and 'for the hallowing of certain conjurations', so as to procure love for his client through magical arts. Coxe also confessed to being part of a network of 'massing priests', which led to the authorities raiding a number of homes, resulting in the arrest of four clergymen, one of who was a former monk. These four malefactors were charged with being involved in a magical plot against Queen Elizabeth.[5]

After the Reformation the illicit texts stored in monastic libraries were also dispersed, resulting in their dissemination into the wider world. These sometimes found their way into the hands of occultists. For example, in the 16th Century the ritual magician Dr. John Dee obtained the numerous occult books held in the library of St. Augustine's (Canterbury). However, despite the increased availability of grimoires, the obscure nature of these magical texts, which comprised of Latin conjurations and complicated procedures, put them beyond the understanding of most lay folk.

5 Young, 'The Dissolution of the Monasteries and the Democratisation of Magic in Post-Reformation England'.

The unique grip ecclesiasts had upon ritual magic was somewhat loosened when the grimoires were translated from Latin into the vernacular. As the knowledge held within became available to a wider audience, ritual magic ceased being the preserve of Latin specialists (such as clerics, monks, and friars), and fell within the grasp of anyone possessing a measure of literacy. Further assisting the democratisation of magic was an increase in the number of educated professionals during the 16th Century, some of whom took a keen interest in the grimoires. These magical practitioners generally came from trades and professions requiring individuals to be at least semi-literate, which ability put them in a higher social position than general labourers. Amongst these learned folk were doctors, teachers, and mathematicians, whose knowledge not only set them apart from common folk, but also lent them an air befitting one trafficking with mysterious forces. Moreover, as knowledge and education was typically accorded an arcane and esoteric quality by poorer folk, those who were well-read were often presumed, however mistakenly, to have some knowledge of the occult arts. Of course, such a reputation had its advantages and was not always unwelcome, as exemplified by the 17th century mathematician and Rector of Albury (Surrey), who was more than content for his flock to regard him as a conjurer.

Individuals who plied magic as their trade were often known as cunning folk, wise men/women, wizards, pellars, or *dyn hysbys*, and such practitioners could be found in towns, cities, and rural districts from the Medieval period onwards. Their art typically combined folk magic with the more learned formulae of the grimoires, and was practiced not so much for spiritual edification but more for the amelioration of the many obstacles besetting man on his journey about the wheel of life. This is to say, whilst the work of magical specialists betrayed a spiritual dimension, it was chiefly practical in its application.

The rise of cunning folk was partly influenced by the Reformation, which religious movement strictly prohibited the clergy from using their priestly powers to intercede in the affairs of man. With the laity's demand for spiritous intervention unchanged, there was thus an increased need for lay conjurors or 'cunning folk' to fill this vacuum, and as a result the magico-religious practices formerly the preserve of priests became secularised and went underground.

With the clergy being for the most part out of the picture, cunning folk became the sole traders of magic for countering bewitchments, cursing thieves, locating lost treasure, curing sickness, divining the future, and providing supernatural protection—tasks the populace once expected priests to fulfil. However, whilst there was a decline in conjuring clergy between the 17th and 19th centuries, a considerable number of rural clerics secretly continued to accede to their parishioners' requests for healing, charming, and incantatory prayers, ostensibly as a means to maintain relevance with their congregations. Such clandestine practices continued well into the 19th century, as attested by the historical record.

Like their ecclesiastical brethren, secular professionals did not consider the magical art to be antithetical to their Christian faith. Illustrative is the 18th century mathematician and cunning man, James Hallett of Chichester (Sussex), who cast astrological nativities and cured diseases. According to Hallett, his magic not only worked through magical artefacts—such as herbal charms, rowan crosses, amulets inscribed with astrological and occult glyphs, pin-pricked hearts, and severed hands—but also 'by the help of God'. Put plainly, he saw no disconnect between his occult practices and his Christian beliefs.

Another magician stressing the importance of a Christian approach to magic was the late 15th century merchant of Augsburg, Claus Spaun. Amongst the many annotations he added to his book of magic was guidance regarding the appropriate angels to call upon, and frequent instruction for the practitioner to kneel devoutly. Implicit is his belief the magician should approach the spirits from a position of humility and piety.[6]

Unlike the clergy, cunning folk were generally more piecemeal in their use of grimoires, conceivably due to their unfamiliarity with the intricacies of ecclesiastical ritual, and a lack of comprehension of the heady mixture of Latin, Greek, and Hebrew used within. Rather than using the texts as complete self-contained systems, they treated them as miscellanies from which to source occult symbols, magical phraseology, and names of power. These disparate elements were then combined

6 Davies, *Grimoires*, p. 40.

together according to personal ingenium in order to create charms, talismans, and ritual operations for the attainment of specific ends.[7]

The cunning folk's methodology of conjuring, spell-craft, healing, and divination may therefore be characterised as a syncretic amalgamation of folkloric and learned (grimoire based) magical formulae, which generally operated within a nominally Christian framework. Testament to the latter is the frequent use of scriptural verses, psalms, and apocryphal biblical narratives within the magical operations. Cunning craft was essentially an art that yoked together differing philosophies in the pursuit of specified magical goals, with the Christian God and his holy retinue of Saints and Angels being just one of many sources of power called upon to empower the practitioner's charms and magical rites.

The cunning folk's magical arsenal not only included operations to lift bewitchments and bring clients health, wealth, and love, but also encompassed methods by which to lay curses. However, whilst witches were popularly imagined to hex people to satiate their intrinsic spiteful nature, the curses of cunning folk were generally motivated by less personal and vindictive reasons, typically being laid on behalf of wronged parties to procure magical justice. This is to say, unlike the wanton and vicious curses hurled by quick-tempered witches, those cast by cunning folk were dispassionate and motivated by profit rather than a desire to do the devil's work, as was thought the case with 'witchcraft' (a term generally used to imply harmful magic).

The punitory maledictions of cunning folk were typically directed as vengeance against thieves, lawbreakers, adulterers, gossips, and other wrongdoers, each of whom would be made to suffer until they had righted their wrong, i.e., returned the stolen goods, stopped spreading malicious gossip, or similar. Cunning folk were also believed to have the power to counter bewitchments, and whilst the church saw little difference between the magic of cunning folk and witches, many lay people considered cunning folk a useful remedy to the problem of 'witchcraft' (*maleficia*). One remedy much-favoured by cunning folk was the witch bottle, which was intended to torture or kill the witch by God's power, thereby working to fight fire with fire. Illustrative is this exemplar from

7 Ibid., 67.

the magical book of William Dawson Bellhouse, a practitioner operative in Liverpool in the late 1850s:

To Hurt or Destroy a Witch

> Cut a little hair of the nape of the neck of the afflicted person or party bewitched, and with parings of finger and toe nails, and some of his blood, and three quarts of his water, a chain of seven links, the middle link to turn down, and the heart of a fresh fowl, and three new needles and three new pins, take them and stick them in the heart a few rusty nails and cards teath, then take three pennyworth of aqua fortis, three pennyworth of vitriol, three pennyworth of french flies [Cantharides], three pennyworth of brimstone, three pennyworth of Dragon's Blood, and in smaller bottles put three drams of each. These must all be put in a strong bottle that withstands fire, or a pan, and boil them on a slow fire until all is consumed.
>
> The chain must be half red hot before it is put in, stir it with a red hot poker five or six times, and whilst turning the poker say these words:
>
> *Witch. Witch. Witch.*
> *I thee burn (or I thee kill) in hell-fire,*
> *If thou does not leave this person and evil turn to thyself,*
> *thou shall feel the wrath of God for ever more.*
> *Amen.*
>
> After this read the 70th Psalm. If a pan is used scrape all well out and bring it at the north side of the house. This will finish it.

This magical charm not only draws upon the power of God and Holy Scripture, but also various principles of folk magic, notably the apotropaic power of iron (the red hot poker), the use of mumia to forge a magic link (the hair, nail parings, and urine), and the power of sympathetic magic (the torturous spines thrust into the fowl's heart, and the idea that heating the bottle will torture the witch). The pins, needles, and rusty nails are included as weapons to harm the witch, which is consonant with the malefic practice of thrusting pins into effigies. The use of barbs in devices for both venomous bewitchments and ameliorative anti-bewitchments demonstrates the neutrality of magical technique—it is the purpose to which the magical art is put, and the moral judgements pronounced upon those actions, that determines whether the deed is seen as fair or foul.

Similar procedures for witch-bottles abound in magical manuscripts and folklore, many of which also call upon God's power for their efficacy. For example, in Sloane 3846, a 17th Century passage describes how the magician should place the urine of the bewitched in a bottle over a fire and insert a pair of red-hot tongs into the bottle whilst cursing the witch and reversing the spell. Another example concerns a cunning man from Wells (Somerset), who told his client to fill a glass vial with urine and add to it seven white thorns, seven black thorns, seven pins, and seven headless nails, whilst saying:

> In the name of Christ I put these pins, thorns, etc. into this bottle, and I wish them not so much to be there as in the heart of the person that has done me this mischief.

The vial was then stoppered and buried beneath the hearth at quarter to midnight.[8]

Whilst the Church officially condemned the activities of cunning folk, laypeople were often at a loss to understand why, especially as many practitioners called themselves 'servants of God' and generally avowed to work in God's name and through His power. In the minds of many, the cunning folk, who sought to make people's life easier through pseudo-Christian charms, were doing precisely the sort of thing clergymen should have been doing more of.[9] Moreover, such was the belief

8 Davies, *A People Bewitched; Witchcraft and Magic in Nineteenth Century Somerset*.

9 Davies, *Popular Magic*, pp. 60–2.

in the Christian nature of this magic that, on occasion, even the clergy sought their services in finding stolen church property.

Sometimes clerics themselves took up the mantle of 'magician', and those who served as cunning men were oft referred to as 'conjuring parsons'. Being godly, these clergymen were thought to have especial power to dominate and control the conjured demons, and to not succumb to their corruptive power. Moreover, being 'men of God', they were arguably the most trusted of the cunning folk. Devon was particularly replete with conjuring clergy, including the early 19th Century parson Reverend William Cummingham of Bratton, who had 'the power' and owned an extensive occult library; the mid 19th Century Reverend Franke Parker of Luffincoat, who was a 'black magician' who could shape-change into animal forms and used occult books to summon demons and spirits; the 17th Century North Devon rector known as 'Parson Joe', who practiced as a consulting astrologer and had various magical powers, including the ability to lay evil spirits; and the Reverend Harris of Hennock, who was a powerful wizard capable of detecting thieves and working love magic.

Another example of a conjuring parson is the Reverend Ruddle, who in the 19th Century helped exorcise a ghostly woman troubling a village near Launceston (Cornwall). He accomplished this by going alone into the haunted field with a forked stick of rowan wood, which he used to trace a circle upon the ground. Within this circle the Reverend drew a pentagram and thrust his stick in the middle where the five points of the star met. He then turned to the North to await the spirit's appearance. When the ghostly woman came, she confessed to having sinned during her earthly life, which had caused her to become trapped on earth, and when the vicar released the troubled spirit she disappeared to the West of the circle and was never seen again. This procedure is unlike the traditional rite of exorcism, and perhaps represents a comingling of liturgical ritual, the learned magic of the grimoires, and folk magic.[10]

Illustrative of the less beneficent ends to which clergyman worked their magic is a case concerning a 15th Century priest from Tournai (Belgium), who was brought before the courts for seducing a girl through magic. He achieved this by drawing her image on a tile using charcoal,

10 Howard, *West Country Witches*, pp. 77–9.

which image he then baptised and sprinkled with holy water. Thereafter he invoked various demons and performed numerous conjurations, which he did in accordance with the instructions in his book of magic.

Another example is Matteo I Visconti, who in 1294 was made an imperial vicar in Milan. In 1320, Matteo, along with Galeazzo I Visconti, was excommunicated by Pope John XXII for the crimes of witchcraft and heresy. The charges included owning a book of magic, of entering into a pact with the Devil, of invoking and working with the Devil, of abusing the sacraments, of using sorcery, and of making an attempt on the Pope's life through the manipulation of a wax doll moulded in his likeness. Also, in 1406–7, a group of clerics were found in possession of a box of books that contained prayers, hymns, and conjurations, which magical formulae they allegedly used against Benedict XIII and the King of France.

Techniques of Christian *maleficia* were also found within a book lent to an Italian woman named Bernardina Stadera, who in 1499 was accused of being 'a charmer, conjurer and procuress.' Bernardina was the lover of a priest, and had borrowed the manuscript from some friars of Modena:

> [It was] a book of paper, handwritten, with a white leather binding, of average size...[When Bernardina used it] she found how to make images and in what way they have to be baptised by a priest to make people love each other, as well as how to curse the mass by saying, "You're lying in your throat" when the priest says, "May the Lord be with you", as she thinks. There was also a conjuration, which included the names of many saints mixed with several names of demons.[11]

Due to their capacity to work magic for both blessing and bane, conjuring clergymen were not only considered to be as powerful as sorcerers, but also just as shady, and for this reason were treated with much the same suspicion and scorn. Indeed, William Thomas, the schoolmaster of Michaelston-super-Ely (Glamorgan), wrote in his diary how the Reverend Samuel Richards (d. 1740), the rector of Barry, was 'a reputed Conjurer, very much dreaded by ye vulgar.'

Victorian Occultism and Imprecatory Magic

DUring the Victorian period, occultism underwent a rather unexpected revival, which was to some extent vivified by an influx of foreign influences, including a burgeoning interest in eastern mysticism and the introduction of spiritualism to Britain by migrant American mediums. Other Victorian occultists instead sought inspiration in the western magical traditions and grimoires, sometimes marrying these influences with eastern spirituality, yet typically professed to use this secret knowledge to change themselves rather than the world about them, i.e., to bring about their own spiritual development rather than obtain material gain.

However, whilst many Victorian occultists embraced a Christian morality to a greater or lesser extent, it did not prevent them occasionally working malefic magic. For example, the Christian mystic and visionary, Dr. Anna Kingsford (1846–1888), occasionally used her occult

11 Davies, *Grimoires*, p. 41.

powers to smite those she considered evil, arguing that whilst black magic was motivated by selfish desires, white magic encompassed anything altruistic, including willing evil people to die. Being a vegetarian and animal rights campaigner, Dr. Kingsford considered these 'evil people' to include vivisectionists who cut and dissected living animals. Indeed, in her diaries she credited herself with killing the French physiologists Claude Bernard (d. 1878) and Paul Bert (d. 1886) through the power of will. Dr. Kingsford also made a magical attempt on the life of Louis Pastor, who was also a keen vivisectionist. However, in this instance she herself fell ill, which she blamed on either her curse rebounding or the influence of 'karma'. Either way, her illness worsened, and she soon thereafter died.

Maledictions in the Grimoires

IN similitude to magical practitioners of other faiths, Christian magicians worked with spirits for purposes fair and foul. These needs were fulfilled by the grimoires, which contained procedures for healing, wealth, love, and rites through which enemies were cursed. Some of these vengeful operations drew upon Catholic liturgical procedures, such as the rite of Excommunication, which already had antecedence as a rite of cursing. One exemplar is St. Adelbert's Curse, which is preserved in Reginald Scot's *Discoverie of Witchcraft*, a text frequently used by cunning folk as a magical source book. This elaborate liturgical curse was said using 'bell, book and candle', and when pronounced against a thief caused them great misfortune. Like other grimoire workings, the operant begins by invoking the various spiritual powers on whose authority he purports to act, and only then proceeds to pronounce and elaborate upon his will, which in this case is to curse, damn, and bind the victim:

Saint Adelbert's Curse or Charm Against Thieves

BY the Authority of the Omnipotent Father, the Son, and the Holy Ghost, and by the holy Virgin *Mary* Mother of our Lord Jesus Christ, and the holy Angels and Archangels, and St. *Michael,* and St. *John* Baptist, and in the behalf of St. *Peter* the Apostle, and the residue of the Apostles, and of St. *Stephen,* and of all the Martyrs, of St. *Sylvester,* and of St. *Adelbert,* and all the Confessors, and St. *Alegand,* and all the holy Virgins, and of all the Saints in Heaven and Earth, unto whom there is given power to bind and loose: we do excommunicate, damn, curse, and bind with the knots and bands of Excommunication, and we do segregate from the bounds and lists of our holy Mother the Church, all those Thieves, Sacrilegious persons, ravenous Catchers, Doers, Counsellers, Coadjutors, male or female, that have committed this theft or mischief, or have usurped any part thereof to their own use.

Let their share be with *Dathan* and *Abiran,* whom the Earth swallowed up for their sins and pride, and let them have part with *Judas* that betrayed Christ, *Amen:* and with *Pontius Pilat,* and with them that said to the Lord, *Depart from us, we will not understand thy ways;* let their Children be made Orphans.

Cursed be they in the Field, in the Grove, in the Woods, in their Houses, Barns, Chambers, and Beds; and cursed be they in the Court, in the Way, in the Town, in the Castle, in the Water, in the Church, in the Churchyard, in the Tribunal-place, in Battle, in their Abode, in the Market-place, in their Talk, in Silence, in Eating, in Watching, in Sleeping, in Drinking, in Feeling, in Sitting, in Kneeling, in Standing, in Lying, in Idleness, in all their Work, in their Body and Soul, in their five Wits, and in every Place. Cursed be the fruit of their Wombs, and cursed be the fruit of their Lands, and cursed be all that they have.

Cursed be their Heads, their Mouths, their Nostrils, their Noses, their Lips, their Jaws, their Teeth, their Eyes and Eye-lids, their Brains, the roof of their Mouths, their

Tongues, their Throats, their Breast, their Hearts, Bellies, their Livers, all their Bowels, and their Stomach. Cursed be their Navels, their Spleens, their Bladder. Cursed be their Thighs, their Legs, their Feet, their Toes, their Necks, their Shoulders. Cursed be their Backs, cursed be their Arms, cursed be their Elbows, cursed be their Hands, and their Fingers, cursed be both the Nails of their hands and feet; cursed be their Ribs and their Genitals, and their Knees, cursed be their Flesh, cursed be their Bones, cursed be their Blood, cursed be the Skin of their Bodies, cursed be the Marrow in their Bones, cursed be they from the Crown of the Head to the sole of the Foot: and whatsoever is betwixt the same, be it accursed; that is to say, their five Senses, to wit, their Seeing, their Hearing, their Smelling, their Tasting, and their Feeling.

Cursed be they in the holy Cross, in the Passion of Christ, with his five Wounds, with the effusion of his Blood, and by the milk of the Virgin *Mary*. I conjure thee *Lucifer*, with all thy Soldiers, by the Father, the Son and the Holy Ghost, with the Humanity and Nativity of Christ, with the Virtue of all Saints, that thou rest not day nor night, till thou bringest them to destruction, either by drowning or hanging, or that they be devoured by wild Beasts, or burnt, or slain by their Enemies, or hated of all men living.

And as our Lord hath given Authority to *Peter* the Apostle, and his Successors, (whose place we occupy), and to us (though unworthy) That whatsoever we bind on Earth, shall be bound in Heaven: and whatsoever we loose on Earth, shall be loosed in Heaven; so we accordingly, if they will not amend, do shut from them the Gates of Heaven, and deny unto them Christian Burial, so as they shall be buried in Asses Leaze.

Furthermore, cursed be the ground wherein they are buried, let them be confounded in the last day of Judgement,

> let them have no conversation among Christians, nor be houseled at the hour of Death, let them be made as dust before the face of the wind: and as *Lucifer* was expelled out of heaven, and *Adam* and *Eve* out of Paradise; so let them be expelled from the day-light. Also let them be joined with those, to whom the Lord saith at the Judgment, *Go ye cursed into everlasting fire, which is prepared for the Devil and his Angels, where the worm shall not die, nor the fire be quenched.* And as the candle, which is thrown out of my hand here, is put out; so let their works and their soul be quenched in the stench of Hell-fire, except they restore that which they have stolen, by such a day: and let every one say, *Amen.* After this must be sung *In media vita in morte sumus, &c.*

The similarity of this malediction to the priestly anathema demonstrates the manner in which clerical formulae came to be used by those outside the priesthood. This particular curse borrows heavily from *Deuteronomy* 28, and evokes various biblical maledictions to draw upon their power, i.e., 'as you cursed X, so may you curse Y'. It also conjures Lucifer in the name of the Holy Trinity, and by power of the Saints, in order to bring the thief to destruction, which is reminiscent of the way demons are constrained by God's power for the attainment of desire in the grimoire tradition. It is also evocative of early anathemas, which often called upon God to command the Devil to punish the victim. Implicit is a belief that the Devil is God's henchman, rather than an antithetical and autonomous principle of evil.

Through the paraphrasing of *Matthew* 16:19, this malediction also evokes the old magical axiom of 'as above, so below', letting whatever the magician binds on earth be bound in heaven, implying the operant's power to enchant or set free by magic.

Another example of a curse from Scot's *Discoverie of Witchcraft* is a charm invoking the Holy Trinity to punish one's enemy by magically beating and maiming them. The spell calls for the use of a hazel wand, which is then struck upon a table, thereby representing the victim being beaten:

> *To Spoil a Thief, a Witch or Any Other Enemy, and to be Delivered From Evil.*
>
> Upon the Sabbath day before sunrise, cut a hazel wand, saying: I cut thee O' bough of this summer's growth, in the name of him whom I mean to beat or maim. Then cover the table and say: ✠ *In nomine patris* ✠ *& filii* ✠ *& spiritus sancti* ✠ *ter*. And striking thereon, say as follows (English it he that can) *Drochs myroch esenaroth* ✠ *betu* ✠ *baroch* ✠ *ass* ✠ *maaroth* ✠: and then say; Holy trinity, punish him that hath wrought this mischief, and take it away by thy great justice, *Eson* ✠ *elion* ✠ *emaris, ales, age*; and strike the carpet with your [hazel] wand.
>
> (Book 12, Chapter 18)

Perhaps the most familiar conception of a curse is that exacted by sympathetic magic, which typically involves the torturous manipulation of an object magically identified with the victim, e.g., piercing a waxen image or melting a candle named for the victim. Whilst this practice is often associated with witchcraft, it is also present in pseudo-Christian magic.

Illustrative is a method preserved in the 15th Century text, *Liber de Angelis* (Book of Angels), which operation is entitled 'Vengeance of Troy' and is used to arouse hatred, cause injury, or bring about a person's death. In the day and hour of the malefic planet Saturn, the victim's image is made in wax, which has ideally been taken from candles lit during a funeral rite. The wax doll is carved with a contorted face to represent the victim in pain, and its feet are placed where its hands should be and vice-versa. The victim's name is inscribed upon the poppet's forehead, which concurs with Agrippa's advice that 'the name of the species or Individuum that the image represents, or for whom or against whom it is made' should be written upon the forehead (*Three Books of Occult Philosophy*), and finds agreement with the scriptural declaration that man is so marked there (*Revelation* 7:13 and 13:16). The name of Saturn is inscribed on the doll's breast, and the seals of Saturn are marked between its shoulders.

With the doll prepared, the magician then calls the spirits of Saturn down to afflict the victim, all the while perfuming it with human bone and hair. The image is then wrapped in a funeral cloth. It is then buried face down in an unclean location. If the magician wishes to harm a specific part of the victim, he wraps that part of the poppet with a strip of funeral cloth and pierces it with a needle. However, if he wishes to kill the victim he drives the needle down into the top of the doll's head, pushing it deep along the spinal axis. To undo the spell, the magician disinters the poppet, removes the needle, anoints the wounds, erases the marks inscribed upon it, and washes it in a fountain.

This magical operation is remarkably similar to a practice described in Scot's *Discoverie of Witchcraft*, where an image is made to hurt or kill a victim:

> ...the hand placed where the foot should be, and the foot where the hand, and the face downward...the like image is made in the form of a man or woman, upon whose head is written the certain name of the party, and on his or her ribs these words, *Ailif, Casyl, Zaze, Hit, Mel, Meltat*: then the same must be buried.

Scot's *Discoverie of Witchcraft* also details the use of poppets to break enchantments. This method involves the backwards recital of *Psalms* 8, 27, 101 (102), and 108 (109), and includes the burial of the effigy to negate the *maleficia*, which is comparable to the burial of a witch bottle to sap an enchantress's power:

> To be utterly rid of the witch, and to hang her up by the hair, you must prepare an image of the earth of a dead man to be baptised in another man's name, whereon the name, with a character, must be written: then must it be perfumed with a rotten bone, and then these psalms read backward: *Domine Dominus noster, Dominus illumination mea, Domine exaudia orationem meam, Deus laudem meam ne tacueris*: and then bury it, first in one place, and afterwards in another.

According to Solomonic tradition, the waxes used for making images should be virgin, being unbleached, uncoloured, and taken direct from the hive, having been put to no other use. In the 14th Century *Hygromanteia* or *Magical Treatise of Solomon*, which text was the precursor of the *Key of Solomon*, instruction is given for the beeswax to be left in a church for three days before being carved, so that it might be present for the saying of a Mass, and after this sojourn the holy names of the Angel Adonai are called upon. However, in the *Key of Solomon* it is the magician him or herself who empowers the wax, and a rite of consecration is given to prepare the wax for its magical use. After invoking various angels to aid in the work, the magus recites several psalms over the wax, and then says an 'exorcism of wax and earth' whilst sprinkling it with holy waters:

Conjuration of the Virgin Earth and Wax

> EXTABOR, NETABOR, SITACIBOR, ADONAI, ON, LAZOMEN, MECHOR, ASMODAH, ASCOBAC, COMTAC, ERIONAS, PROFETAS, ALIOMAS, CONAMAS, PAPIEREDOS, OSIANDOS, NARBONIDAS, ALMAY, CACAY, COAQNAY, EQUEVAT, DAMNAT, VERNAS, COMPARES, SCIES, GERADES, SERANTES, COPHILADES—Ye Angels of God be present, for I invoke ye in my work, so that through you it may find virtue and accomplishment. Amen.

Following this a series of psalms are to be recited, namely:

130 "Lord, my heart is not haughty"
14 "Lord, who shall abide in thy tabernacle?"
101 "Hear my prayer, O Lord"
8 "O Lord our Lord, how excellent"
83 "How amiable are thy tabernacles O Lord"
67 "Let God arise, let his enemies be scattered"
49 "The mighty God, even the Lord, hath spoken and called"
53 "Save me, O God, by thy name"
71 "Give the king thy judgements, O God"
132 "Behold, how good and how pleasant"

113 "When Israel went out of Egypt, the house"
125 "When the Lord turned against the captivity"
46 "O clap your hands, all ye people"
45 "God is our refuge and our strength"
21 "My God, my God, why hast thou forsaken me?"
50 "Have mercy upon me, O God, according to thy loving kindness"
129 "Out of the depths have I cried unto thee, O Lord"
138 "O Lord, thou hast searched me, and known me"

After this the magus says the following exorcism over the wax or earth, whilst asperging it with the Holy Water of Arte:

Exorcism of the Virgin Earth and Wax

> I exorcise thee, O Creature of wax (or of Earth), that through the holy name of God and his holy angels thou receive blessing, so that thou mayest be sanctified and blessed, and obtain the virtue which we desire, through the most holy name of Adonai. Amen.[12]

12 *The Key of Solomon* Chapter 18, Book 2.

According to Solomonic tradition, the needles used to prick the wax image are also consecrated by magical formulae:

> I conjure thee, O Instrument of Steel, by God the Father Almighty, by the Virtue of the Heavens, of the Stars, and of the Angels who preside over them; by the virtue of stones, herbs, and animals; by the virtue of hail, snow, and wind; that thou receivest such virtue that thou mayest obtain without deceit the end which I desire in all things wherein I shall use thee; through God the Creator of the Ages, and Emperor of the Angels. Amen.

Following this Psalms 3, 9, 31, 42, 60, 51, 130 are repeated.

Perfume it with the perfumes of the Art, and sprinkle it with exorcised water, wrap it in silk and say:

> DANI, ZUMECH, AGALMATUROD, GADIEL, PANI, CANELOAS, MEROD, GAMIDOI, BALDOI, METRATOR, Angels most holy, be present for a guard unto this instrument.

A spell employing a wax doll against enemies is given in A. E. Waite's *Book of Black Magic and of Pacts*, which work of hate and destruction is purportedly taken from a manuscript copy of the *Key of Solomon*. After preparing the wax image, it is fumigated and inscribed with the needle of art, after which the following is said over it:

> VSOR, DILAPIDATORE, TENTATORE, SOIGNATORE, DEVORATORE, CONCITORE, ET SEDUCTORE. O all ye ministers and companions, I direct, conjure, constrain and command you to fulfil this behest willingly, namely, straightway to consecrate this image, which is to be done in the name of [name] that as the face of the one is contrary to the other, so the same may never more look one upon another.

The image is then buried in a place with 'evil odours', especially those of Mars, such as sulphur and asafœtida, and left there for one night, after having been asperged with holy water.[13]

Illustrating the ecclesiastical use of grimoires and wax dolls is an attempt made on the life of Pope Urban VIII, which was undertaken at the behest of Giacomo Centini, the nephew of Cardinal d'Ascoli, that his uncle might attain the pontiff's seat. In 1663, Centini asked a hermit adept in the occult arts, and with close familiarity with demons, to apprise him of his uncle's prospects. The hermit told Centini that whilst Cardinal d'Ascoli would succeed Pope Urban VIII, the current incumbent had many years left to live, but he could magically shorten the Pope's life if Centini so desired. Seduced by the hermit's scheme, Centini enlisted the aid of several clerics, including Bernardo di Montalto, who had a reputation for making wax images of women and melting them above flames to procure love.

Having fashioned a wax effigy of the Pope, complete with regalia, the clerical malefactors anointed and consecrated the doll with a Mass of the Holy Cross. Using hemp spun into a thread by a virgin, they laid a magic circle upon the floor of a room within Centini's palace and lit a fire at its centre. Then, using a knife they had forged, inscribed, and consecrated in accordance with the instruction found in the *Key of Solomon*, they held the wax effigy over the brazier's flame, calling forth demons to aid in the work. At the rite's conclusion, infernal spirits were invoked to reveal whether the endeavour had been successful, but as no spirit appeared or answered, they assumed their ceremony had failed. Two more attempts were afterwards made, each of which was held in a vineyard at night, but these also met with failure. Frustrated at the lack of success, the hermit said they needed to find seven priests to undertake the rite together, one of who would have to be sacrificed to enforce the spell. However, growing suspicion and gossip soon brought the clerics' plot to the attention of Rome, and the malefactors were brought to trial; Centini was beheaded, the hermit and another sorcerous cleric were burned alive, and the rest were given severe punishments.

Magical proxies were not always anthropomorphic in form, as demonstrated by a magical operation in a 15th century book of magic, where

13 A. E. Waite, *The Book of Black Magic*, pp. 292–4.

two stones are used to kindle hatred between two parties. At the heart of the spell is an act of analogical magic, wherein the two parties are represented by two shiny round stones taken from a river, each being named for an individual and buried beneath the threshold of the one it represents. After seven days the two rocks are retrieved before sunrise and cast into a fire, saying:

> I conjure you most inimical spirits, by the glory of the everlasting God, to sow and arouse as much hatred between [name] and [name], whose names are carved here on these stones...

The stones are then taken out of the fire and placed in a pale of cold water, where they are left under a clear sky for three nights. On the fourth night they are removed and fumigated with sulphur, saying:

> I conjure all you hateful and malignant, invidious and discordant demons...to arouse at once between [name] and [name] as much hatred as there was between Cain and Abel. Arouse them and inflame them so much that one cannot stand to see the other, and one will afflict the other with immeasurable hatred, as a rebel. May all love, affection, fraternity and concord be removed from them; let them be turned to enmity and utter hatred.

This conjuration serves to evoke the hatred between the biblical brothers, Cain and Abel, and may be considered an act of analogical magic, i.e., 'as there was enmity between Cain and Abel, let there be enmity between [name] and [name]'. Moreover, just as words and names of power are used to evoke the virtues they signify, so too are biblical events recalled in order to evoke the powers that caused their un-enfoldment, which power is then sublimated to the spell's specified objective. In this instance the operant evokes the power of hatred driving a wedge between Cain and Abel, which is used to drive the two victims apart.

After the conjuration the stones are stored away, and on the following night are brought out and repeatedly bashed together to represent the two parties coming to blows, saying:

> I do not smash these stones, rather I smash [name] and [name], whose names are written here, so that one will at once afflict the other and they will torment each other from now on with unconditional hatred.

This is done thrice every day and night for several days. Alternatively, if the magician desires to separate the two parties, the operant is instructed to bury the stones in two separate places, saying:

> As I have separated these stones, thus may [name] be separated from [name], and may they be as distant as these stones.[14]

The practice of symbolically burying two proxies apart from one another is also found in Book 1, Chapter 5 of the *Picatrix*, where through *similia similibus* two lovers are caused to be separated, even as burying them together causes the pair to fall in love.

Another curse combining analogical magic with a biblical narrative is a spell from a Swedish Black Book. Having put three glowing coals in a hand-mill, the operant grinds them three times clockwise, saying:

> Just as I drag this mill around clockwise, so too do I drag the thief back who has stolen from [name], justly as the traitor Judas who sold his master our dear Saviour Jesus Christ for 30 pieces of silver, and he justly bore the same money back again, so shall you, damned person and thief who took goods from [name] and has robbed them; with shame and timidity return them back again, or this curse will be and attack you as is written in King David's Psalm 109.'

This is to be done in the morning before the sun has come up, and on an empty stomach.[15] The symbolic component is represented in the draw-

14 Richard Kieckhefer, *Forbidden Rites*, pp. 72–4.

15 Thomas K. Johnson, *Magical Representations in the Swedish Black Art Book Tradition'*, p. 325.

ing round of the mill, which works to 'draw back' the thief, whilst the narrative formula evokes the blood money of Judas.

A similar coercive spell 'to get back what a thief has stolen' is found in the *Black Books of Elverum*, which pair of handwritten grimoires were discovered in an attic in Norway, and were likely written between 1790 and 1820. The ceremony involves putting hot embers in a mustard seed grinder on a Monday morning and grinding them counterclockwise with the left hand whilst saying the following words five times, "Hafel. Ageltor. Hafel." It is written that, 'as the embers burn, so will that person's heart burn, and never stop burning before he brings back again the goods that he has stolen.' The embers are then placed on the floor and stepped on with the right foot, whilst thrice repeating the following incantation, "Like this ember shall your heart be. Just like this ember under my foot. In the name of the Father, and the Son, and the Holy Spirit."[16]

Another spell to harm one's enemy by proxy is found in the *Grimorium Verum*, and like the curse doll is exacted by point of nail. The rite involves digging up an old coffin from a graveyard, removing the nails from it, and saying:

> Nails, I take you that you may serve to turn aside and cause evil to all persons whom I will. In the name of the Father, and of the Son, and of the Holy Spirit. Amen.

The magician then drives one of the nails into the enemy's footprint whilst saying *Pater noster upto in terra*, meaning 'Our Father who art on earth'. The nail is then hammered into the footprint using a stone, whilst saying, "Cause harm to [name] until I remove thee." Herein the victim's footprint serves as a proxy of the victim, which is established by virtue of the magical law of contagion. Once cast, this spell can only be lifted by removing the nail whilst saying:

> I remove thee so that the evil which thou hast caused to [name] shall cease. In the name of the Father, and of the Son, and of the Holy Spirit. Amen.

16 Rustad, *The Black Books of Elverum*, pp. 63–7.

Another maledictive formula exacted by point of nail is found in Scot's *Discoverie of Witchcraft*, and works to identify a thief by causing him unbearable pain in his eye. Magic against thieves is a common staple of the grimoires, and was perhaps considered licit by virtue of the fact it was aimed at individuals who had sinned:

To Put Out The Thieve's Eye

> Read the seven Psalms with the Litany, and then must be said a horrible prayer to Christ, and God the Father, with a curse against the thief. Then in the middle of the step of your foot, on the ground where you stand, make a circle like an eye, and write thereabout certain barbarous names, and drive with a cooper's hammer, or add into the middle thereof, a brazen nail consecrated, saying: *Justus es Domine, justa judica tua*. Then the thief shall be bewrayed [made known] by his crying out.
>
> (Book 12, Chapter 12)

By driving the nail into the picture of the eye, the operant intends to magically assail the guilty party, who crying out in pain is thereby identified. In this particular instance the act of sympathetic magic is aided and empowered by the use of barbarous names, the seven penitential Psalms, and imprecatory prayer.

More explicit instruction regarding this ritualistic procedure is found in numerous Latin and English texts treating of this operation under the name of 'Eye of Abraham'. Whilst the rite is technically given as a means of identifying a thief, it works by causing the victim so much pain they have no choice but to confess their guilt, or else spend their remaining days in pain, which essentially renders it a curse.

In one 16th Century English grimoire the operation is entitled, 'The Eye of Abraham, for proving persons guilty of theft that they confess their guilt.' It describes how a diagram of the eye is to be drawn, and how the pupil is to be surrounded by a triple-banded circle. In the outer circle the name *Iesus Saluator* ('Jesus the Saviour') is written, and in the inner circle the magician writes, *Iesus siens rerum occultarum & manifestarum versus purgatory, ocuins nomine precioso* ('Jesus knowing hidden and manifest things, the truer purifier, O you whose name is precious'). The following charm is then said over the drawing:

> I conjure all of the lookers on this eye, and all of them that is in this thing to be guilty of and is beholding of this eye; I conjure them by the virtue of the Father and of the Son and of the Holy Ghost, and by all the names of God, Alpha and Omega + and by all of the apostles, and by all the evangelists and martyrs and confessors and by the holy elements, and by St Mary, the mother of our Lord Jesus Christ, and by all their works, and all them that be guilty of such things which is gone, and all they that behold this eye so fast, strike it on his eye, by the virtue of the holy names of our Lord Jesus Christ, before said, that it never cease till his eye be out, or give answer and for them to be brought again, and God for his mickle might, that right as I smite this nail on this place, that we may believe that all virtue that is in these words aforesaid, may form to pain and to confusion.

Then, as the nail is hammered into the eye the magician says:

> *Rabat, vel Rabas, Selarinum Reatonay seliare Reatony facite apperere qui illam Rem, furatus sine de qua querimus*", meaning, 'Rabat (or Rabas), Selarinum Reatonay seliare Reatony, make appear that thing stolen, or other thing which we seek.[17]

This particular grimoire contains another magical operation against thieves, where the image of an eye is instead drawn on a wall, and the names *Malkeo*, *Nabbasr*, *Colkeranon*, and *Battenayer* are written about it. Whilst pressing the sharp end of a copper nail against the pupil, the magician says:

17 Harms, Clark & Peterson, *The Book of Oberon*, pp. 492–3.

> Malkeo, Nabbasr, Colkeranon, and Battenayer, *Conjiuro vos spiritus ut faciatis furem apparere, et appereries os suum et recognoscere furum quod querimus*

This translates as 'I conjure you, O spirit, that you make the thief appear who we are seeking, and make his face be shown and recognised.'[18]

The 'Abraham's Eye' formula to punish a thief by piercing their eye is also found in an early 4th Century Greek papyrus. The operant is instructed to paint an eye on parchment and draw a circle about it, which is to be inscribed with the names of four angels. The parchment is then taken to a public place where the thief might be present, and a prayer is made to God asking for assistance, with various spirits being invoked by name. The point of a knife is then driven into the eye, or else a hammer is used to bang a key into it, which causes the thief to cry out in pain, thereby revealing his identity. Another variant simply instructs the operant to draw the eye on a wall and strike it with a hammer.

A 6th century Greek version of this thief identifying charm, which also sought to inflame the guilty party's eye, involves taking the herb *khelkbei* and *bugloss*, pressing out the juice, burning the crushed leaves, and mixing the resultant ashes with the juice. This mixture is then used to anoint and write the following upon a wall:

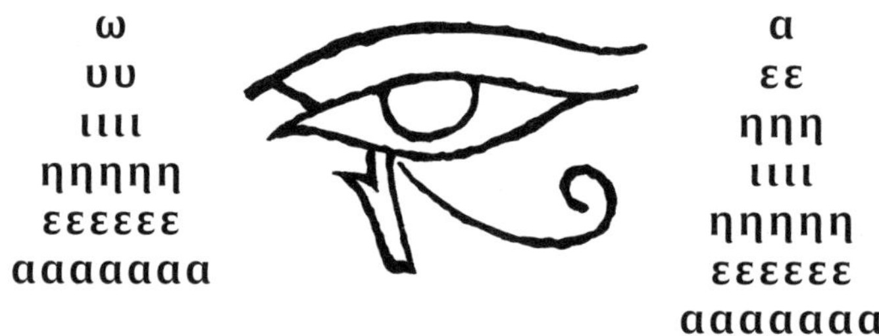

Herein the *utchat* ('Eye of Horus') is flanked by an arrangement of vowels. In Gnosticism the seven vowels are representative of the seven archons or planets, which in combination represent the universe, and are thus powerful adjuncts in magic.

18 Ibid., 357–8.

A hammer is then cut out of a piece of wood and used to strike the image whilst pronouncing this spell:

> I adjure thee by the holy names, render up the thief, who has carried away such [and such] a thing Khalkhak, Khalkoum, Khiam, Khar, Khroum, Zbar, Bêri, Zbarkom, Khrê, Kariôb, Pharibou, and by the terrible names αεεηηηιιιιοοοοουυυυυυωωωωωωω.
>
> Render up the thief who has stolen such [and such] a thing: as long as I strike the eye with this hammer, let the eye of the thief be smitten and inflamed until it betrays him.[19]

Another version from a 4th Century Greek papyrus calls for an onion to be placed on the image of the eye, and rather than hammering it to 'put out the eye', the magician instead says, "Thief, let the onion bite you." By this method the operant uses sympathetic magic to cause the thief's eye to become sore and inflamed, even as gasses from cut onions cause eye irritation, and through this affliction the thief's identity is revealed.

Interestingly, Scottish witches used a method very similar to 'Abraham's Eye' to exact their curses. After reciting imprecatory Psalms backwards, the witch drew an image of an eye upon the ground using their left foot. Around this image they then wrote various 'barbarous words of power' and names of demons. With this done the curse was exacted by striking a brass nail into the middle of the eye using a hammer purloined from a blacksmith's forge.[20]

A similar method 'to put out the eye of a thief' is also found in the Norwegian *Black Books of Elverum* (c. 1800). The practitioner is to attend church on a Sunday morning, taking with them some chicken fat, mercury, and man's blood. During the service these ingredients are surreptitiously blended together to form a dough, which dough ostensibly gains its power by the sacrilegious deed of sublimating a religious ser-

19 Budge, *Egyptian Magic*, pp. 57–8.
20 Michael Howard, *Scottish Witches and Warlocks*, p. 121.

vice to magical purposes. This mixture is then used to draw an eye on the table, with these words being placed around it:

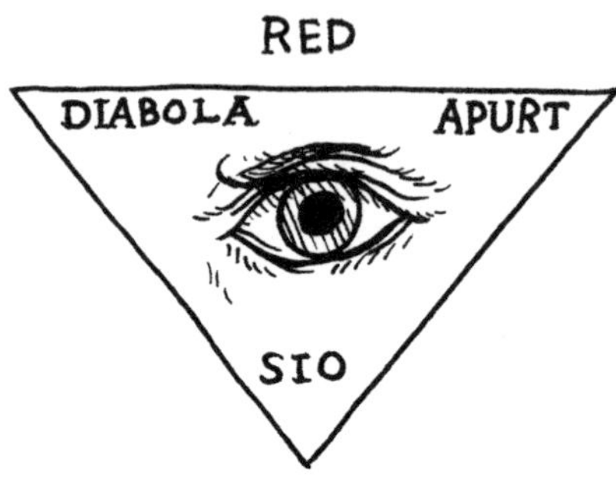

The practitioner then obtains a copper nail that has been forged on a Sunday morning before the sun goes up, and made by three blows from a hammer in the Devil's name. This nail is set against the drawn eye, and three blows are struck with the same hammer whilst saying, "Satan, Beelsebub, Bellial, Ashtarath, and all the devils that are in Hell."[21]

Interestingly, the books contain another rite drawing upon the motif of immolation, which is similarly intended to 'point out a thief'. The practitioner is to smear a mirror with a mixture of incense and Easter candles, marjoram, holy water, and breast milk at 9:00 PM on a Thursday. A heart is then drawn in the centre of the mirror, and certain words are written around it, including the phrase, 'Jesus Christ's side and heart were pierced through with a spear.' This mirror is then hidden in a dark room for three nights, after which the operant returns to the mirror, wherein he will see the thief's name and whereabouts.[22]

The Black Books of Elverum also include a rite to 'make a thief come back', which draws upon the power of both God and the Devil. The practitioner takes a coin in their hand and on a Thursday night goes to the side of a river or stream that runs from south to north, and says:

> I command you, sun and moon, that you do not shine on this thief.

21 Rustad, *The Black Books of Elverum*, pp. 73–5.
22 Ibid., 27–9.

> I call upon you, Lucifer and all your followers.
> And I adjure the Devil from Hell.

The coin is then thrown into the water, presumably as an offering, and the following is spoken:

> Do not give this thief either rest, relaxation, or tranquility before he brings back to me that which he has stolen from me.
> God, do not let this thief have any rest or tranquility, day or night, morning or evening.
> Let his heart burn like a burning ember that can never be extinguished,
> And let him be as restless as a wave on a wild beach, until he has returned the goods he has stolen from me, to the spot or place it was taken from.
> This shall fully happen in the Devil's dreaded name that lives in Hell's abyss.
>
> *(The names of Hell's ten princes can be added here.)*[23]

This coercive charm wherein the thief cannot have any rest day or night is rather reminiscent of the magical use of *Deuteronomy* 28. It also draws upon the symbolism a burning ember to represent the thief's burning heart, which calls to mind those Nordic rites wherein actual burning embers are ground in a hand-mill to evoke the grinding of the thief's heart.

The *Black Books of Elverum* also include a curse against witches, which spell is read on a Thursday evening over salt and running water by one over whom evil has been cast, or who has been bewitched:

> Today, which is D.N.N. [the Lord's] day over all Christendom, I read these words with God's power and might, and with Jesus Christ's finger.
> I point to wherever bewitching has been performed by

23 Ibid., 67–71.

> witches, using bird or fish bones, by the north or the south wind, by soil or by mountain or water sprite, on purpose or by accident, in or outside, in food or drink, sitting or lying riding or driving.
> I hold today your liver and lungs, your heart and tongue, your hands and feet, and your cursed heart's roots.
> You shall never do more harm to any person.
> I say this with the highest power and might in the name of the Trinity.
> You shall remit yourself to these words as salt for the running water.
> Amen.
> After this the Lord's Prayer is recited three times.[24]

This charm hints at the paths by which witches were thought to exact their curses, namely through bones, winds, spirits, or bewitched victuals. It also contains some interesting shades of *Deuteronomy* 28 in its attempt to encapsulate all eventualities, invoking the words 'on purpose or by accident, in or outside, in food or drink, sitting or lying, or riding or driving.' The charm further supposes the practitioner's will to be as one with that of God, with the practitioner's finger even becoming as one with that of Jesus, which is to say their finger is ridden by the son of god.

Another spell the book gives for 'protection against witches' takes the form of a narrative charm evoking the spectre of the generational curse, which reads as follows:

> Jesus and the Virgin Mary walked over a wide bridge. There they met the witch, Lede [the evil one]. "Where are you going?" Jesus asked. "I'm going to a farm to injure people, goats and sheep, horses and cattle to the ninth generation." "No," Jesus said, "you shall go away, you horrible bag, over this brook. You shall burst in the very roots of your heart and in your cursed feet." In the name of the Trinity.

24 Ibid., 29–31.

After this the individual is to say the Lord's Prayer three times. Interestingly, in the manuscript the end of the prayer is marked with the sign of the upside-down pentagram, ostensibly to evoke the protective power ascribed to the pentagram.[25]

More mundane than the curse of a witch is the physical violence perpetuated by man-upon-man, and to this end, the *Black Books of Elverum* also contain a charm drawing upon religious powers to smite an enemy. This narrative charm is intended to dull the sword of an enemy in war, and is comparable to the use of biblical verses, both actual and apocryphal, to gain magical aid in combat. To achieve the magical effect, the practitioner is to say:

> "Our Lord, He went on a gentleman's expedition. He dulled all the drawn swords. 'All drawn swords,' he said, 'I take from them point and edge, so they cannot injure, neither woman nor man.' Peter with his sword did the Devil's mischief. In the name of the three." Then recite the Lord's Prayer.[26]

In addition to operations for attaining specific ends, as exemplified by the aforementioned curse rites, the grimoires also contain instruction for conjuring angels, demons, fairies, ghosts, and other spirits to accomplish the magician's desire. These desires might include the procurement of visions and revelatory knowledge, or spiritous intervention in pursuits of health, wealth, love, and revenge.

These rites of conjuration typically require the use of specialist apparatus, such the magic circle, triangle of art, pentacle, sword, wand, knife, and trident, which accoutrements frequently have correlatives within the magical practices of pagan antiquity. Yet, despite these historical 'pagan' associations, the majority of the grimoire's rites were 'Christianised', albeit in a manner considered heretical by the orthodoxy.

Grimoiric conjurations typically open with a declaration to summon a specific spirit or group of spirits, such as "I conjure and evoke you, O [spirit's name]." This is followed by an enunciation of the various sacred

25 Ibid., 32–3.
26 Ibid., 53.

powers by whose authority the conjuration is empowered, e.g., "by the power of the Holy Trinity, by the holy names by whose power you are bound, by the four evangelists, the twelve apostles, and the three magi, by the power of all the holy saints, by the power of the blessed virgin Mary, and by the power of heaven and earth and all things in them." These powers are essentially the engine driving the conjuration, and connote the operant's belief that all things are under the dominion of the Christian God, and may thus be commanded in His name. Finally, the magician declares the task the spirit(s) are charged with carrying out. When a curse, this could be something along the lines of, "that you may sow and stir up hatred between [name] and [name]" or, "that you may plague and torment [name], and cause great misfortune to befall them."

Books of magic often contain a list of spirits and the uses to which they may be put. This is especially true of the Solomonic grimoires, which draw upon a mythos from the *Testament of Solomon* (circa 1st–5th century) relating how God gifted King Solomon a signet ring marked with a magical seal that had the power to command spirits. With this ring Solomon conjured up numerous demons, commanding each to reveal their powers and the words by which they could be controlled. These are purportedly the self-same spirits whose names and powers are listed in the Solomonic grimoires, along with instruction for their evocation, and the words and signs by which they are commanded. After forcibly extracting this information from the spirits, Solomon:

> ... bound and sealed up the spirits and their legions in a brazen vessel...and by it Solomon gained the love of all manner of persons and overcame in battle, for neither fire nor water could hurt him.
>
> *Ars Goetia: The Lesser Key of Solomon*

The Solomonic grimoires thus exhort all who desire to work the system to follow the wise king's example, commanding the spirits using his God-given Seal, and using a brazen vessel as a locus of spirit manifestation:

> ...thou mayest command these spirits into the Vessel of Brass in the same manner as thou dost into the Triangle... [so] that thou dost forthwith appear before this Circle, in this Vessel of Brass, in a fair and comely shape.
>
> *Ars Goetia: The Lesser Key of Solomon*

THE uses to which the spirits can be put are many and varied, and amongst their copious powers are the ability to bring death, destruction, misfortune and illness, to cause discord and battles, to bind the actions of enemies, to make people impotent and sterile, and to effectuate the destruction of houses and property. However, even when working towards such nefarious ends, the spirits are always commanded and constrained by God's permission and aid, and invoked by means of His sacred powers.

Illustrative is a cursing rite from A. E. Waite's compendious *Book of Black Magic and Pacts*, which concerns the sowing of discord through the bewitchment of food—a method more traditionally associated with witchcraft. During the day and hour proper to the work, specifically those of Saturn or Mars, the magician makes the following adjuration over the food, which works to conjure and bind the named discordant spirits through the power of God:

> Where are ye, SOIGNATORE, USORE, DILAPIDATORE, and DENTORE; CONCISORE, DIVORATORE, SEDUCTORE, and SEMINATORE? Ye Who sow discord, where are you? Ye who infuse hatred and propagate enmities, I conjure you by Him who hath created you for this ministry, to fulfil this work, in order that whensoever N [the person's name] shall eat of like things, or shall touch them, in whatsoever manner, never shall he go in peace.

The bewitched food is then given to the victim during the hour of Saturn or Mars.

In some instances, the malefic work is overseen by angelic forces rather than constrained demons. For example, if a magician wished to depopulate a house, cause bloodshed, illness, destruction, or inflict other types of harm he could make an image using red copper or red wax on a Tuesday and suffumigate it with pepper, which work is under the angelic power of Samael. Or, to cause enmity, he could make an image of saturnine lead on a Wednesday and suffumigate it with altast, which work is under the angelic power of Michael.

Maledictions worked by holy agency are also contained in *The Book of Abramelin*, which grimoire outlines a demanding schedule of prayer and chastity that, successfully undertaken, gives the magi 'knowledge and conversation' with their guardian angel. Once contact with this guardian angel has been established, the magician may ask the spirit to evoke, bind, and command the twelve kings and dukes of hell to carry out their every desire, whether fair or foul. To help attain their desire the magician uses one of the many talismanic magic word squares contained within *The Book of Abramelin*, which include those 'to excite every description of hatred and enmity', those to cause 'loss and damage', and those to bring ruin to towns and houses.

These imprecatory magic squares are based on various words expressing maledictive intent, such as SINAH, meaning 'hatred', SELAK, meaning 'to cast down and prostrate', NOKAM, meaning 'vengeance', BINIAM, meaning 'in affliction', QARAQAK, meaning 'thy rending asunder', and QELADIM, meaning 'those who creep in insidiously'. A particularly baleful square is the CASED square, which:

> ... should be either buried or concealed in places where the persons we wish to harm are likely to pass by; or, if possible, we can touch them with the Symbol

C	A	S	E	D
A	Z	O	T	E
B	O	R	O	S
E	T	O	S	A
D	E	B	A	C

4

Christianity and the Lay Tradition of Magico-Religious Cursing

BEFORE THE MODERN period, few amongst the general populace could afford the cost of bringing a prosecution before the courts of law, and even those who could had little faith in the justice system, which typically favoured the noble and wealthy. It is thus unsurprising that the poor and downtrodden turned to God and His holy retinue for spiritous aid in the procurement of divine justice. Moreover, of all reprisals against wrongdoers, God's curse was considered the most terrifying of all.

In order to solicit God's aid in delivering justice, some parishioners approached the local priest to lay curses on their behalf. In the 15th century, for example, Thomas Perne of Gilden Morden (Cambridgeshire) approached his local vicar after becoming a victim of theft, and in response the vicar stood at the pulpit and announced his intention to curse the thieves unless the stolen goods were immediately returned.[1] However, after the Reformation, when the clergy were prohibited from such deeds, many took matters into their own hands, even though the church deemed these undertakings unorthodox and illicit. These lay attempts at 'magical' justice were particularly suited to the resolution of issues concerning revenge, familial disputes, adultery, usury, and salacious gossip, which the Church and courts had little interest in.

1 Thomas, *Religion and the Decline of Magic*, p. 599.

As the majority of the populace were nominally Christian, those seeking preternatural aid in the obtainment of blessing, protection, healing, knowledge, and revenge, generally called upon powers drawn from the retinue of Christian spirits, specifically God, Jesus, Mary, the saints, apostles, magi, and angels. Moreover, the methods they used to secure this spiritous intervention were often predicated upon, and aped from, the priestly rites of the church. In consequence, these lay curses often took inspiration from priestly maledictions and biblical tradition, much as self-blessing, healing, and protection was sought through the use of prayers, tapers, chrism, and holy waters. Through such practices the people's faith became a practical and everyday part of life, which helped ease the problems bedevilling their daily round.

Whilst many modern Christians consider it antithetical to use a 'positive' and godly force for the obtainment of a 'negative' effect, the practice of using prayer and holy items to evoke curses was once quite acceptable. Indeed, whilst modern societies now place much emphasis on restorative justice, in earlier times the concept of 'justice' had a very different and much more Old Testament feel.

The actions of most people, regardless of personal faith, are influenced by what they (rightly or wrongly) consider to be right and proper, and when people seek to harm another it is usually because they believe the person(s) concerned have wronged them, their kith and kin, or society in general. Therefore, when a person or group had violated the accepted 'Christian' code of conduct, it seemed quite natural to appeal to God or one His holy retinue to recognise this 'wrong' and smite the offender(s) through numinous intercession. Confirmation of this is found in the prevalent motivations of lay curses, which include such 'un-Christian' behaviours as lawlessness, injustice, adultery, harassment, immorality, violence, theft, vice, ungodliness, and defilement of sacred space. However, whilst it was considered somewhat justifiable to call God's wrath down upon those who had 'sinned', it was deemed reprehensible to do so without proper justification. Indeed, many believed their imprecations to be invocations of God's Judgment, which would rebound unless motivated by a just cause.

In surveying the incidence of cursing in early modern Britain, it is notable that the vast majority were made by the poor and dispossessed against the rich and strong. And, during the 16th and 17th Centuries, the curses pronounced by the impoverished and injured were considered of especial potency. Particularly feared were the widower's curse and the curse of a fatherless child. As one 18th Century English poet avowed, 'if anyone's curse can effect damnation it is not that of the Pope but that of the poor'. This meant that whilst the poor and infirm were vulnerable to the capricious whims of the ruling classes, when all else failed they had a means of preternatural retaliation.[2]

Imprecatory Prayers

ONe of the simplest methods for laypeople to visit revenge on those who had wronged them was through imprecatory prayer. However, whilst imprecatory prayers were typically motivated by injustice, some believed they took effect regardless of the supplicant's motivations. For example, in 1397 the Bishop of Hereford was informed that whatever curse Alison Brown of Broomyard pronounced, God always put it into effect.

Scriptural basis for imprecatory prayer is found in Jesus' cursing of a fig tree, which caused it to wither away (*Mark* 1:12–14, 11:20–25 and *Matthew* 21:18–22). After this deed, Jesus told his disciples of the power of prayer to effect change, and how they too could achieve miraculous effects through the power of faith:

> Truly I tell you, if you have faith and do not doubt, not only can you do what was done to the fig tree, but also you can say to this mountain, 'Go, throw yourself into the sea,' and it will be done. If you believe, you will receive whatever you ask for in prayer.

This stance is evocative of the magical use of will and belief in sorcery, which sorcerous application is adeptly expressed by Andrew Chumbley in his work, *The Azoëtia*—'Do not believe a thing because you think it to be true, but to make it so.'[3]

2 Thomas, *Religion and the Decline of Magic*, pp. 604–5.

3 Chumbley, *The Azoëtia*, p. 327.

Examples of imprecatory prayer are found throughout scripture and the saint's hagiographies, and the practice was once much favoured by clerics. From the Middle Ages onwards, it was also commonly used by lay people. One medieval exemplar concerns a widower and her children, who were forced from their home by a man named John Tregoss, who abused his position as a trustee of a Cornish estate to take the land for his own. To remedy this injustice the evicted family made daily supplications upon their knees, adjuring God to visit retribution upon Tregoss and his descendants. So severe were the ensuing misfortunes that even as late as the reign of Charles II a descendent of Tregoss, a clergyman named Thomas Tregoss, spent many hours praying for the curse to be lifted.

However, during the Reformation, clerics and common folk alike were forbidden to invoke and unleash heavenly wrath upon their enemies, or to pray for their downfall. To enforce this ruling, officers of the Church visited local churches to discover whether parishioners had been cursing their neighbours or goods. Yet, in spite of the church's best efforts, the practice endured.[4]

The popularity of imprecatory prayer is attested by church records, which are replete with examples of laypeople who, believing themselves wronged, went down on bare knees to pray for vengeance. For example, during a kirk session in Mid Calder (West Lothian, Scotland) in 1705, Barbara Aikin was accused of having

> ...gone down on her bare knees at the place where the stocks lies and cursed [Lord] Torphichen and wished his family extinct, and wished all the woes and curses she could mind might come on the family, saying, "the curse of the everlasting God come on him and his wife."[5]

In the Isle of Man, curses made whilst kneeling were considered of magnified potency. This practice is exemplified in a court case from 1713, when one Henry Quay fell to his knees mid-trial and bitterly cursed his opponent using 'such imprecations as are not fit to be repeated'. For this

4 Thomas, *Religion and the Decline of Magic*, p. 600.

5 Ibid., 602–6.

outrageous act the presiding judge, Deemster McYlrea, gave Henry over to the Church to be disciplined, which resulted in his imprisonment in the Bishop's dungeon at Peel.[6]

When praying for vengeance, female supplicants often prayed with their hair loosed and hands raised to the heavens. In the Isle of Man the loosening of hair was associated with the *Skeab Lome*, meaning 'the bare broom' or 'the besom of destruction.' This fearsome curse of annihilation was intended to curse the hearth, being the very heart of the household, and by extension the family gathering about its mystic centre. This is to say, like an apple made rotten at the core, the accursed taint was to spread outwards and spoil the whole.

To exact the *Skeab Lome* the operant faced the door of the victim's house and uttered their imprecation, all the while making the gesture of sweeping with a broom. This mimetic act served to represent the enemy being swept away, much as British folklore contended the sweeping of

6 David Craine, 'Sorcery and Witchcraft in Man in the 17th and 18th Centuries', *Journal of the Manx Museum*, IV, 1939, Nos 59 & 60, pp. 122–4 & 139–40.

a house with a blossomed broom in May swept the head of the house away. Comparable is the use of 'sweepers' by West Country witches, which were used to 'sweep bad or good luck away from one to another place or person, or vice-versa.' These sweepers were made of a variety of natural materials, but most popular were those formed of white goose feathers tied together with thin red thread.[7]

The spoken element of the *Skeab Lome* varied in its form, but fairly representative is this example from 1744:

> "May the Besom of Destruction come upon thee thyself, upon they hearth, upon the health, upon thy possessions, and upon thy children!"

Another example from the parish of Kirk Patrick from 1735 went:

> The Besom of Destruction upon the man belonging to the Cleigh, a fireside without offspring, and an empty desolation with neither root nor seed![8]

To enhance the potency of the *Skeab Lome*, the operant uncovered her hair so it fell loose and free. According to scripture, it was sinful for women to pray with their hair loose; 'Every woman who prays or prophesises with her head uncovered dishonours her head...' (1 *Corinthians* 11:5). A woman's hair was also accorded a certain power to bewitch men and allure evil spirits. Indeed, many Christians and Jews maintained the fallen angels were tempted to earth by the unveiled hair of the daughters of men, and the authors of the *Malleus Maleficarum* (1486) asserted demons were attracted by women's beautiful hair.

In accordance with such beliefs, Christian women covered their heads when worshipping in church or public, and because female hair was associated with sinfulness and temptation, most women wore some sort of head covering when in mixed company. This was especially true of married women, who generally only allowed their hair to be seen by

7 Object Number 357; The Museum of Witchcraft and Magic, Boscastle.

8 Craine, 'Sorcery and Witchcraft in Man in the 17th and 18th Centuries', *Journal of the Manx Museum*, IV, 1939, Nos 59 & 60, pp. 122–4 & 139–40.

their husbands. Yet, whilst young unmarried women were permitted to have loose hair, those that did were often regarded as being immodest, indecent, of poor breeding, and of loose morals. The exception to this was in Scotland, where women went bareheaded or bedecked with red ribbons until marriage, after which they would wear a coif.

The act of uncovering the hair during imprecatory prayer thus served to emphasise the apostatic nature of the accursed deed, with the power released from this oppositional act being sublimated to the attainment of the individual's desire. It may also have served as an abasement of the self in order to make a *clamour*, which degradation was accentuated by the individual's prostration on bare knees.

The loosening of hair during imprecatory prayer may also relate to the folk belief that women's hair contained a witchen power, which could be used to bewitch men and to allure spirits that might aid in her magical work. Illustrative is the belief witches cursed and enchanted victims by shaking their hair at them, which is widely attested in Scotland. For example, on 21st March 1633 the spae-wife, Bessie Skebister, was brought to trial in Kirkwall (Orkney) for bewitching one Margaret Mudie by sitting down (perhaps kneeling), removing her curtch (a kerchief-like head covering) and shaking her hair loose at the victim. After this bewitchment Mudie suffered great pains, which progressively worsened. As a result of the trial Bessie was sentenced to be strangled and then burned at Gallow Ha'. Another example concerns Isobell Young, who was convicted of taking off her courche (head-covering) in order to cause the misfortunes befalling one William Meslet.[9]

The relationship between a witch's power and his or her hair is also attested in allegations made in 16th century Scotland, which relate how the devil preached from the pulpit of St. Andrew's church (North Berwick, Scotland), telling his witchen disciples they could not be harmed, 'so long as their hair was on.' Because of such beliefs, those accused of witchcraft were typically shorn to render them powerless, which practice is avowed by Sir James Frazer:

> Here in Europe it used to be thought that the maleficent powers of witches and wizards resided in their hair, and

9 Dalyell, *The Darker Superstitions of Scotland*, p. 451.

> that nothing could make any impression on these miscreants so long as they kept their hair on.[10]

The act of unbinding the hair essentially worked to liberate the woman's witching power so it could flow freely and allure the spiritous agencies that assisted her. The loosening of the hair also symbolised a rejection of society's strictures, and invokes a wild and primal state wherein the liberated individual becomes as one with the unbridled and natural forces of life and death. As the act of freeing the hair was considered tantamount to the rejection of the authority of church and state, those praying with unbound hair were marked out as 'other', and were typically glossed as witches working against the dictates of societal convention and the natural accepted order of things.

The ceremony of the kneeling malediction was typically performed in public and before witnesses, such as in a crowded street or churchyard.[11] An example of the latter is found in the Hereford diocesan court records of 1598, and concerns a man who cursed his victim by kneeling in a churchyard (i.e., a place of death) whilst 'praying unto God that a heavy vengeance and a heavy plague might light upon him and all his cattle.' The desire for plague to befall an enemy and their cattle is a common component of Biblical curses, clerical maledictions, and formulas of excommunication.

The prayer's spoken element typically took the form of an extemporised entreaty to God and his holy retinue, who were exhorted to visit various punishments upon the wrongdoer. Typically, the individual would pray to God to shorten their victim's life, cause 'an evil death' to light upon them, wither their limbs, rot their tongues, burn their houses, kill their children, destroy their goods, visit plague upon their cattle and crops, and curse their descendants—all maledictions to be found in scripture and hagiography. One popular curse, which evoked a specific Biblical malediction, was to call for 'God's curse and all the plagues of Egypt' to be upon the victim and their descendants.

10 George James Frazer, *Folk-Lore in the Old Testament: Studies in Comparative Religion, Legend, & Law.*

11 Thomas, p. 605.

In some cases, the prayer took the form of a specific formula rather than an inspired imprecation. For example, in 1634 a woman from Winwick (Oundle) claimed to know a specific prayer to shorten a man's life. Another formulaic prayer is the following curse, which was remembered by an old man from South Wales in 1858, and like other extant exemplars betrays the influence of *Deuteronomy* 28:

> I curse thee! I curse thee! I curse thee standing, walking, riding, driving, running; awake and asleep; at morning, noon, and night; both eating and drinking, going out and coming in.
>
> I curse all that is made and done by thee, all that is touched by thee.
>
> May thy crops and fruit be cankered, thy flocks and herds diseased; thy daughters be ailing, and thy sons be maimed!
>
> May thou die thrice accursed, and may thy descendants for seven generations reap the harvest of this my curse!
>
> Then shall thy house be the home of the raven and the bat, the snake and the viper!

This particular curse was to be uttered in Welsh, and the old man named several families and old houses around Wales that had been victim to its malefic power. Spoken curses were widely feared in Wales during the 18th and 19th Centuries, and were laid on people and places by priests, witches, and those having righteous indignation for a wrong suffered. Once spoken, the curse was thought to last at least seven years, and could descend on the victim at any time during that period. In some parts, it was believed the curse could even last until the 7th generation.[12]

Imprecatory prayers are also presumed to have drawn upon Latin phraseology, *voces magicae*, and/or glossolalia, as suggested by a case from 1617, when Joanna Powell of Westhide 'did curse John Smith, one

12 Marie Trevelyan, *Folklore and Folk Stories of Wales*, 1909.

of the churchwardens...in Welsh language, kneeling down upon her bare knees and holding up her hands, but otherwise [using] words he could not understand.'

Curses could also be inserted into other prayers as part of the individual's on-going dialogue with God. Illustrative is the case of John Story, who was executed for treason in 1571 for daily cursing Queen Elizabeth I during the saying of his mealtime grace.

When rightly pronounced, imprecatory prayers were believed to have a devastating effect upon their victim. Demonstrative is a case from Essex, where in 1596 a woman who had been asked to cure a man's sick wife with medicine instead got down on her knees, and, after many curses and evil speeches, prayed the sick woman 'might never be cured, but might abide the extremist torments that ever was abidden.' After the curse the sick woman is said to, 'hath lain and yet doth lie in great misery and can find no ease.'

The belief that imprecatory prayers were fulfilled by holy agency and not the devil is attested by the plethora of exemplars making appeal to God and his heavenly retinue. For example, in 1557 Sibyll Dews of Somerset prayed to God and the Virgin Mary that one Edward Tyrell would never prosper in body or goods. Also, in 1614 one Catherine Mason cursed a man named Robert Davies, whom she believed to be responsible for her husband's death, by 'praying to God that his house, his children, and all he had were one wild fire.' Similarly, in 1630, Margery Bluck of Hereford cursed one Mary Davies by 'praying to God that an evil end might come of her', and in 1634, Isabel Oxley got on her knees and made a prayer of execration to call divine judgment upon her enemy, saying "God's plague and God's curse light upon thee and thine beasts, and may God never let they or anything thou hast prosper or do well" (*Acts of the High Commission...Durham*, 1858).[13]

However, in effectuating curses without the church's authority, imprecatory prayers were at risk of being interpreted as witchcraft. Illustrative is an excerpt from Thomas Cooper of Christchurch's *The Mystery of Witchcraft* (1617), which treats of a woman who, desiring revenge on her enemies, had resorted to 'invocating upon her bare knees (for so the manner is) for the vengeance of God.' However, even though the

13 Thomas, *Religion and the Decline of Magic*, pp. 602–6.

woman's plea was directed to God, Cooper determined the malediction was actually effected by Satan.

Another example of an invocation of God's vengeance becoming conflated with witchcraft concerns Elizabeth Lowys of Waltham (Essex), who was brought before the courts in 1564. She was accused of using witchcraft to lame her husband, kill two pigs out of spite, and of blasting a woman and a child, the latter of whom was left writhing with its body twisted. Lowys frequently used imprecatory prayer to maim her enemies, and during the trial was asked to answer for the following act of blasphemy:

> ...whether she in her yard or house, kneeling, standing, or lying flat, spoke these words: "Christ, my Christ, if thou be a Saviour, come down and avenge me of my enemies, or else though shall not be a saviour."

This appeal to God not only constitutes a cursing prayer, but also bears similarity to a clamour, as she threatens God that if He does not curse her enemies she will turn away from Him. It was conceivably assumed that in spurning God she would turn instead to His counterpart, the Devil. Lowys was also asked about the prayer's gestural element (whether she prayed whilst kneeling or lying flat) which suggests certain postures were associated with the ritual act. Notably, both kneeling and lying flat were popular postures for the making of clamours.

Another instance of imprecatory prayer being interpreted as witchcraft concerns a case from 1662, which centred on two neighbours from Herefordshire named Philip Benny and Mary Hodges, who were embroiled in a protracted quarrel. Things came to a head when Philip accused Mary of witchcraft, alleging that after her kith and kin had retired to bed she did:

> ...take the andirons out of her chimney, and put them cross one on other and then she falls down upon her knees and useth some prayers of witchcraft...She then makes water [urinates] in a dish and throws it upon said andirons and then takes her journey into her garden. This is her usual custom night after night.

Philip claimed Mary had undertaken this deed to curse his son Richard and their cattle.

Whilst Philip interpreted Mary's prayers as being those 'of witchcraft', the act of forming a cross by laying andirons across one another, and then kneeling whilst praying, is more suggestive of a pseudo-Christian practice. Mary was also accused of being 'a swearer and blasphemer of God's word', which suggests her 'witchcraft' was no more than the non-licit use of God's name.

Particularly intriguing is the use of urine during the rite, which conceivably relates to the practice of heating urine as an anti-bewitchment charm. Alternatively, in throwing urine on the crossed andirons, Mary may have intended the humiliation of the cross, thereby evoking the abasement of holy icons during the making of a clamour.

Another instance where pseudo-Christian imprecatory prayer might have been interpreted as witchcraft concerns the cursing of a hated Laird's offspring by the Auldearn coven (Scotland). Their curse was carried out using effigies of his children, which were made from clay mixed with water from a holy well. The women then knelt down with their loosened hair hanging over their faces and their hands upraised, praying to their 'Devil' that the Laird's children would die and his house would be left without an heir. Whilst Gowdie confessed to witchcraft, it is difficult to know at this distant juncture whether these prayers were really directed to the Devil, or whether they were instead imprecatory prayers to God that were re-imagined as prayers to the Devil due to their malefic intent and the use of effigies.

After these women made their accursed prayers, each clay doll was scorched over a fire until black and hard. The dolls were then removed from the flames, swaddled in black cloth, and placed in a cradle. The following day, and every day thereafter until the children died, the dolls were removed from the cradle, unwrapped, washed in holy water, and re-subjected to the blackening flame.

Vengeful prayers were also muttered over holy candles in the church and home, even as lay people prayed over the same to procure healing and blessings. An example of this custom was collected in America by the mid-20th Century Anglican minister, Harry M. Hyatt:

> ...if you have enemies [to be] removed, you could get a black candle and put it in a dark place and burn it. Burn it for nine nights and ask the Lord to [re]move them, and he'll [re]move them.

Hyatt's informant claimed this practice was especially efficacious if the operant fasted and got down on his knees to pray to the Lord, as was commonly done in Britain. This is to say, the individual intended for the prayer to be effectuated by God and not some demonic agency.

Whilst historical information regarding the content of imprecatory prayers is scant, one detailed example is preserved amongst the Irish curses in Dr. Douglas Hyde's *The Religious Songs of Connacht*, and was discovered by the Irish priest and scholar, Father Patrick Dineen, in a manuscript belonging to one Mr. O'Byrne of Castleknock. The curse, which is lengthy and descriptive, is pronounced against three enemies—Bruadar, Smith, and Glinn—and fervently appeals to God and Christ under a variety of Gaelic appellations, including The King of Angels, The King of Brightness, and The Son of the Virgin. The twenty-fourth verse of this imprecatory prayer also references an awareness of the cursing psalms, whose maledictions are called down upon Bruadar, Glinn and Smith:

> Each one of the wicked three,
> Who raised against me their hand,
> May fire from heaven come down and slay,
> This day their perjured band,
> Amen!
>
> May none of their race survive,
> May God destroy them all,
> Each curse of the psalms in the holy books,
> Of the prophets upon them fall.
> Amen!

Within this prayer curse the Lord is invoked in his guise of the King of Friday, the King of Saturday, and the King of Monday, which three days were considered especially unlucky in Irish folklore. Indeed, the Irish poem, 'On Friday', cites a number of calamitous biblical events supposedly occurring on a Friday; it was the day Adam sinned, the day he was sent from Paradise, the day hell opened, the day Cain killed Abel, the day the Flood was sent on the world, the day Christ was crucified, the day briars and thorns were made, the day Herod killed the children, the day St. Peter and St. Paul were crucified, and the day John the Baptist was decapitated. In Galway there is also a proverb declaring, 'The beginning of Friday and the end of Saturday are bad.' Another Irish belief avows three specific Mondays to be especially accursed—the first Monday of April, when Cain was born and killed his brother Abel, the second Monday of August, when Sodom and Gomorrah were destroyed, and the last Monday in December, when Judas the betrayer of Jesus was born.[14] In appealing to the Lord as King of Friday, Saturday, and Monday, the curser essentially worked to invoke God in his vengeful aspect.

Poetic maledictions with a religious element are also found in Scotland, as illustrated by the following examples from Volume 2 of Carmichael's *Carmina Gadelica*:

A Malediction

There came two out,
From the City of Heaven,
A man and a woman,
To make the 'ōisnean'.
Curses on the blear-eyed women,
Curses on the sharp-eyed men,
Curses on the four venomous arrows of disease,
That may be in the constitution of man and beast.

The opening lines of this malediction are somewhat reminiscent of a charm for burns, which begins, 'There were two angels, who came from the North'—although in other variants the angels number three and/or come from the East. The reference to blear- and sharp-eyes may connote the evil eye as an originator of disease, and perhaps suggests the charm was intended to curse otherworldly agents of disease. Lending weight

14 Douglas Hyde, *The Religious Songs of Connacht: A collection of poems, stories, prayers, satires, ranns, charms, etc.*, pp. 219–221.

to this theory is another charm from the *Carmina Gadelica*, which references keen and peering eyes in relation to 'fairy darts' and 'the swift arrows of the furies':

Charm

Peter and James and John,
The three of sweetest virtues in glory,
Who arose to make the charm,
Before the great door of the City,
By the right knee of God the Son.

Against the keen-eyed men,
Against the peering-eyed women,
Against the slim, slender, fairy-darts,
Against the swift arrows of furies.

Two made to thee the withered eye,
Man and woman with venom and envy,
Three whom I will set against them,
Father, Son, and Spirit Holy.

Four and twenty diseases in the constitution of man
        and beast,
God scrape them, God search them, God cleanse them,
From out thy blood, from out thy flesh, from out thy
        fragrant bones,
From this day and each day that comes, till thy day on
        earth be done.

This charm against wrongdoers was collected from a travelling tinker named Isabella Chisholm, who was in possession of a number of other spells, charms, runes, and hymns, including the following exemplar, which invokes vengeance in God's name:

The Wicked Who Would Do Me Harm

The wicked who would do me harm,
May he take the [throat] disease,
Globularly, spirally, circularly,
Fluxy, pellety, horny-grim.

Be it harder than the stone,
Be it blacker than the coal,
Be it swifter than the duck,
Be it heavier than the lead.

Be it fiercer, fiercer, sharper, harsher, more malignant,
Than the hard, wound-quivering holly,
Be it sourer than the sained, lustrous, bitter, salt,
Seven seven times.

Oscillating thither,
Undulating hither,
Staggering downwards,
Floundering upwards.

Drivelling outwards,
Snivelling inwards,
Oft hurrying out,
Seldom coming in.

A wisp the portion of each hand,
A foot in the base of each pillar,
A leg the prop of each jamb,
A flux driving and dragging him.

A dysentery of blood from heart, from form, from bones,
From the liver, from the lobe, from the lungs,
And a searching of veins, of throat, and of kidneys,
To my contemnors and traducers.

In the name of the God of might,
Who warded me from every evil,
And who shielded me in strength,
From the net of my breakers,
And destroyers.

Comparable to the use of imprecatory prayers are written curses, which are tantamount to 'written prayers' and demonstrate how the power of word is expressed through both speech *and* the use of letters and symbols. The motif of the written curse is found in *Zechariah* 5:1–4, where the prophet Zechariah looks to the sky and sees a vision of a flying scroll, which he is told is a written curse going forth across the face of the land. On the one side of the scroll is a curse against those who steal, and on the other is a curse against those who swear. It is written the scroll will enter the house of any who commit the aforementioned transgressions, and 'will spend the night within that house and consume it with its timber and stones.'

Like their spoken counterparts, curse texts from the late antiquity onwards frequently make appeal to scriptural and hagiographical miracles, thereby accessing the divine powers described therein. Particularly popular were appeals to episodes from the Old Testament, wherein God's judgement and wrath is unleashed against various oppositional figures, including Cain, Herod, Pharaoh, and the Assyrian army. In appealing to Holy Scripture the would-be curser makes clear their intent to draw upon heavenly aid rather than demonic agency, which, in the mind of the operant at least, renders the curse permissible in Christian society.

Written curses were deposited in churches, graveyards, shrines, and holy wells, which is comparable to the way Græco-Roman *defixiones* (curse tablets) were treated. More advantageously, they could also be sent anonymously to a victim's home, thereby delivering the curse into the victim's sphere of existence, even as poppets and accursed artefacts were believed more efficacious when buried or hidden in the victim's home or land.

One example of a written curse is the anonymous letter received in April 1889 by a young yeoman who farmed some land near Ashburton

(Devon). As the curse was published only a few years after its discovery, the names and place were changed to maintain the victim's anonymity:

An Injured One's Curse

Nikson, repent, the time is near,
When before thy God you shall reappear;
Thy life has been a wicked race,
So pray to God to give you grace.
Thy bonnie bride, when she has borne
A son, shall leave thy home forlorn;
And when the first-born son is won,
And *Furzdon* goes to first-born son;
It's then my curse shall have its sway,
From that time forth to Judgement Day,
Without some act of special brand,
To a despised and suffering man,
You wipe away by glorious deeds
The act that makes my heart to bleed;
When this is done my curse is o'er,
No *Nickson* its weight shall bear no more.

In *Notes and Queries for Somerset and Dorset* (1895) it was reported the victim's wife gave birth to a son the following May. However, tragedy struck and the child died that very September, which greatly upset the young yeoman, causing him to fall ill for some time after his son's sudden bereavement.[15]

Whatever events transpired prior to penning this malediction, the author of the curse evidently felt they were the wronged party, and that God would concur with their own personal judgement. Moreover, even though the curse targets the yeoman's son rather than the yeoman himself—an innocent party—the imprecator obviously believed their curse was a just and warranted response to right the perceived wrong. Any justification for targeting the victim's child was perhaps founded upon the scriptural precedent set by the numerous generational curses within the Bible.

15 *Notes and Queries for Somerset and Dorset*, 1885, pp. 157–8.

Rather than sending written curses to the victim's home, some wronged parties instead concealed them within their own homes as defensive and retaliatory amulets. These exemplars typically cursed any who wished harm upon the occupants and/or their property. Illustrative is a written charm found hidden in a crack of a wooden beam in a cottage in Chink (near Clwyd, Wales):

> In the Name of God arise and scatter mine enemies,
> Let them be as The Dust before The Wind,
> And the Angel of the Lord scattering them.
> Put on the whole Armour of God that we may be able
> to stand against the wiles of the devil.
> Dei gratia illum quod Sacrument Ingrato.

This curse, which calls upon God to smite one's enemies, draws heavily on biblical texts, most notably *Psalm* 35, which is a prayer for delivery from one's enemies, and *Ephesians* 6:11 ('Put on the whole armour of God, that ye may be able to stand against the wiles of the devil.'). It was written on a pentagon shaped piece of paper, which was perhaps intended to evoke the protective powers ascribed to the pentagram.

Other written curses earnestly combined biblical passages and Latin phrases from pre-Reformation liturgy with astrological symbols and occult glyphs. This suggests lay folk considered the fusion of Christian and 'occult' philosophies as being somewhat acceptable, and did not necessarily consider it a transgression of their Christian faith. This was presumably because the symbols were taken from grimoires operating within a Christian framework and/or having alleged Christian provenance, such as those purportedly written by the likes of King Solomon or Moses. Illustrative of such curses is an inscribed lead tablet found in a cupboard at Wilton Place (Dymock, Gloucestershire) in 1892. The tablet is marked at the top with the victim's name, 'Sarah Ellis', which has been written backwards, ostensibly to evoke retrogressive powers. Beneath it are various astrological and occult glyphs evoking the moon, which are followed by an invocation calling upon eight spirits, the first of whom is linked to the moon. The invocation asks:

> ...make this person banish away from this place and country, amen. To my desire, amen.

In the culminative use of the binding phrase, 'Amen', the curse is lent the likeness of a prayer.[16]

The Vengeful Saints: Petitions, Cursing Stones, Holy Wells, Murderous Icons, and Ritual Reversal

WHilst some prayed directly to God to invoke divine judgement upon enemies, others petitioned a panoply of saints and folk-saints, which powerful spirits served as emissaries between man and God. It was to these go-betweens the needy oft-repaired when seeking numinous aid, whether for healing, protection, reassurance, knowledge, guidance, fertility, or cursing. Because saints were once mortal, and therefore sympathetic to the human condition, many found them easier to reach out to and converse with than a nebulous and almighty non-incarnate God. The immanence of the saints was reinforced by the array of iconography and statuary depicting them, which made the saints tangibly present and accessible in churches, saintly shrines, and the home. Through interaction with these icons, and the intercession of the depicted saint, the common folk were afforded a practical way of seeking God's aid in day-to-day concerns.

The Christian custom of seeking aid from saints, apostles, and members of God's angelic host finds its inversion in the manner witches sought to satiate their desires through the intercession of fairies, ghosts, familiars, demons, and other members of the Devil's infernal horde. Yet, whilst the powers supplicated are antithetical to one another, the desired boons are identical, namely those of healing, protection, love, knowledge, and cursing.

The saints' wonder-working powers were known to the common folk through the tales told of the miracles they performed during their lifetimes. These miracles not only included the ending of droughts,

16 Ralph Merrifield, *The Archaeology of Ritual and Magic*, pp. 147–8.

eruption of springs, curing of disease, and fructification of things barren, but also malefic phenomena, such as withering limbs, bringing plague, and striking down dead those who 'deserved' it, which is to evoke the saint as a holy warrior, avenger, and righter of wrongs.

Since the earliest days of Christianity, it was believed saints could exert these self-same powers even in death, which is attested by the many miracles and visions procured after their martyrdom. Indeed, many saints were as active (if not more so) in death as they were in life, which posthumous miracles helped affirm a belief in the doctrine of resurrection. These mighty and holy spirits of the dead were thus entreated by Christian folk for blessings, healing, and protection, and also as patrons of cursing for the procurement of vengeance.

The belief saints granted desires both fair and foul is not isolated to Britain. Indeed, in *Croyances et Légendes du Centre de la France* ('Beliefs and Legends of the Centre of France', published 1875), the French ethnographer Germain Laisnel de La Salle remarks how, 'the saints carry their complaisance [desire to please] for us so far, that our desires, even the most criminal, find an assistance in the heavens.' As an example he cites Saint Sequayre (possibly related to Saint Seçaire), to whom the Basques prayed when desiring their enemies to slowly wither away and die. Another example concerns a French man who prayed at the shrine of St. Martianus at Bourges (France) after his cattle was stolen. As a result of this appeal to saintly power, the thief 'lost his way and like someone out of his mind, returned to the place from which he had set out'.[17] A similar effect was secured by the spells of witches and cunning folk who sometimes sought to cause their victims to become lost or wander astray.

The saints could be petitioned at churches, shrines, holy wells, and points in the landscape dedicated to them. Such places were sometimes locales where important events in the saint's mortal life had played out, or points where saints had made visionary appearances after death. More conveniently, saints could also be petitioned within the domicile through the use of holy icons and statuary.

The petitions made at these locales characteristically conformed to the three-fold formula of summoning, petitioning, and the offering of

17 Bartlett, *Why Can the Dead Do Such Great Things*, p. 402.

votive 'payment'. The summoning could be as simple as kneeling before the saint's statue and addressing them by name, whilst the petition typically took the form of an extemporised plea or a formal prayer for effect. In petitioning the saint a transactional relationship was established—the saint becoming as patron and the petitioner as client—and as with any transaction, certain obligations were required of both parties: the saint provided the miracle, and the petitioner provided the 'payment'. This payment or votive offering served to seal the pact, and could take many forms, including the making of pilgrimage, the doing of 'good deeds', the offering of coins, flowers or incense before the saint's image, and the making of donations to the church for the upkeep of the saint's shrine.

Another form of offering is the *ex-voto*, from the Latin *ex voto suscepto*, meaning 'from the vow made', which connotes an offering given to the saint in fulfilment of a vow. The original custom was to leave wax candles in the saint's shrine, which offertory practice obtained from the 4th Century to the Middle Ages. From the 6th Century onwards, votive candles were sometimes made equal in height to the person needing help, which forged a symbolic link between the individual and the candle. Other times, the wick was cut to the length of the person and then folded back on itself several times, which afforded a candle of a more wieldy length. From the 9th Century onwards, blocks of wax equal in weight to the individual began to be left, which could later be melted down to make candles benefitting the church, and by extension its patron saint. Around this period people also began to offer candles conforming to the 'measure' of stricken animals.

The 9th Century also marks the inception of the better-known practice of making *ex-votos* in the form of figurines (usually of wax), which simulacra were made to represent the person as a whole, or elsewise the individual body part the saint was to heal. From the 12th Century onwards, figural *ex-votos* were also made into the likeness of animals, boats, and other objects requiring saintly aid. Where these votive offerings were left in a church or shrine dedicated to the saint, they served as a testament to their powers and accomplishments, ensuring all future visitors would be assured of the saint's mighty power.

The placement of figural and anatomical votives in saintly shrines is evocative of older pagan customs. For example, the practice of carving wooden feet and wooden men for making vows at pagan holy sites was condemned in a canon from the Diocesan Synod of Auxerre as early as the late 6th Century. Around the same time Gregory of Tours wrote how his uncle had found a temple in Cologne where, 'barbarians... sculpted limbs from wood whenever one of them was afflicted with pain.' Wooden simulacra were also left by 'pagans' at sacred points within the landscape, as attested by St. Pirmin in his early 8th Century work, *Dicta Abbatis Pirminii, de Singulis Libris Canonicis Scarapsus* ('Words of Abbot Pirminius, extracts from the Single Canonical Books'); 'Do not make or place limbs of wood at crossroads, trees, or anywhere else, for they can offer you no healing'.

Whilst Christian *ex-votos* were offered in exchange for healing and other virtuous boons, the notion that figural representations and measured candles retained a magical link with their votary gave rise to the idea they could also be misused by those of a sorcerous persuasion. It was feared that just as simulacra were crafted to obtain healing, so too could they be made and used for the purposes of causing harm, which practice was a devilish inversion of the Christian custom. Some scholars suggest the increasing popularity of figural *ex-votos* actually served to re-invigorate the belief in the art of manipulating wax effigies for malefic effect.[18]

Another once common method of petitioning saints involved the use of a person's measure, which was variously taken as being their height, their width (the distance between fingertip and fingertip of their outstretched arms), or the length of their belt or girdle. Being concordant with the individual's proportions, this measure was thereafter treated as a symbolic representation of the person. Implicit is the belief that a person's proportions codify their essential nature, evoking the idiom, 'the measure of a person'.

Measures were sometimes taken using braided thread, which were then dipped in wax to make a votive candle. With the person's measure at its core, the taper became a veritable effigy of the sick—the wick representing their spinal column and the wax their flesh. A comparable principle underpins the use of the Paschal Candle as a symbolic repre-

18 'The Curious History of Wax Figurines in Medieval Europe' by Kati Ihnat and Katelyn Mesler, *Entangled Histories*, pp. 138–147.

sentation of Christ; the wick His soul, the wax His flesh, and the flame His divine spirit.

These candles were treated much like *ex-votos* and were typically lit before a saint's image, with prayers being made to the saint(s) for healing, anti-bewitchment, or numinous aid. As the taper burnt down, so was the illness or bewitchment hoped to diminish with it.[19] For example, in the *Life of St. Gotthard*, it is related how a 12th Century priest helped an impoverished mother by measuring her dying child with flax to make a votive candle. This candle was placed before St. Gotthard, whose intercession was sought to make the boy well.

Being symbolic representations of the individual, these candles were tantamount to poppets, and were sometimes used for darker arts, thus demonstrating the manner in which curative rites were perverted into rites of cursing. The candle, with the victim's measure as its wick, was typically struck with pins and burnt before saintly icons, all the while muttering imprecatory prayers. As the candle wax melted, so too was the victim hoped to waste away, which analogical deed is synonymous with the custom of melting pin-struck wax poppets over a flame.[20]

Illustrative of the imprecatory use of candles is a case concerning Johanna Benet, who on the 10th and 11th June 1490 was brought before the Commissary of London for attempting to waste away a man by burning a candle named for him. As 'a *sortelega*, and making use of acts of *sortelegium*', Johanna was accused of measuring the man's height and making a candle of the same length, which she offered in front of a *coram imagine* ('statue or painting'—most likely that of a Saint), so that the victim would waste away with the melting of the candle.[21] A 5 or 6-foot candle would have been expensive, which suggests Johanna (or her client) was either relatively wealthy, or else the braided thread was folded upon itself several times before being dipped into the wax, thereby affording a more wieldy candle, which practice is attested in the historical record.

It is unlikely idle spite would be sufficient motivation to undertake such an involved malefic practice, which suggests victims were instead

19 Merrifield, *The Archaeology of Ritual and Magic*, p. 90.
20 Murray, *The God of the Witches.*
21 Maxwell-Stuart, *The British Witch*, pp. 84–5.

commended to the saints' judgment to procure retributive justice against those who had offended or harmed the individual or their kith and kin.

In Britain, saintly intercession was also secured by bending a coin whilst making prayers and entreaties to the saint. The coin was usually bent over the head of the individual or animal the saint was being asked to help or heal. However, other times the coin was magically identified with the needful party by circling it over their head, or using it to trace the sign of the cross upon their forehead. Alternatively, it was simply pointed in the direction of the person, place, or object the prayer was intended to affect, which deed could be done more surreptitiously.

Whilst this use of coins is typically associated with benefic ends, it also served in the making of imprecations. Illustrative is a practice from Ireland, where curses were placed upon individuals by taking a silver sixpenny coin, bending it, and placing it in a church, saying, "May I bend a coin on the Holy Ghost on you!"[22]

The coin itself was a votive offering made to seal the pact, and after the rite of entreaty was left at the saint's shrine or holy well. Pliable coins, which had been bent as part of the petition, were rendered useless in this world, which caused them to become a sacrament offered wholly to the otherworldly saint. Comparable are the bent and mutilated weapons historically cast into bodies of water as votive offerings to 'pagan' spirits and gods.

Sometimes, points within the landscape became identified with a saint, which association was typically incepted because important events in the saint's life occurred there, or the saint's spirit appeared and/or worked miracles there, or a votary of the saint dedicated the locale to them. These places became regarded as hot points where the saint's power could be accessed, often for the purposes of achieving miracles synonymous with those performed by the saint in their lifetime. One such locus is Colm Cille's bed, which is a large rock atop *Mulla na Lap* ('the Summit of the Bed') near Carrickmore, and according to legend St. Colm Cille made his bed in the large crevice within this rock. As late as 1866 this rock was used for a cursing rite known as 'sweeping Colm Cille's bed', which was undertaken between sunset and sunrise

22 Power, *The Book of Irish Curses*, p. 35.

(midnight) and involved sweeping the floor of the crevice using a shirt or chemise, depending on whether a man or woman.[23] Considering the many maledictions associated with Colm Cille in the hagiographies, it is unsurprising a landmark associated with him should become a place of cursing.

Another place of malefic virtue is the site of an old church in Kilcummin, which was allegedly founded by St. Cuimin, and contained a sixty-metre-long flagstone known as *Leac Cuimín* ('the Stone of Cuimin') that was reputed to have lain over the saint's grave. The wardens of the site were the Maughan family, who allegedly descended from a man who rescued the infant saint from drowning, and they alone had the right to wield St. Cuimin's power for blessing or bane. They brought these twain powers to bear by administering earth from the saint's grave for curative purposes and using his gravestone for putting curses on wrongdoers and slanderers.

To procure a malediction the petitioner had to fast for fifteen days, after which they approached the Maughan family, who would carry out the rite for a fee, which served as an offering to the saint. The rite involved making circumambulations around the nearby well of St. Cuimin, whose waters were reputed to be curative, and culminated in the Maughan guardian 'turning the stone' against the enemy.[24] The practice came to an end during the early 19th Century, when the stone was removed and built into the wall of the cathedral at Ballina (County Mayo) for 'certain weighty reasons', more specifically, to prevent it being used for superstitious purposes.

Stone turning was also a component of 'The Curse of the Twelve Bridgets', which malediction was carried out against a landlord named O'Hare, who had unjustly evicted several tenants at Loughrea (County Galway). To redress this injustice twelve girls each buried a sheaf of corn on O'Hare's land, and afterwards repaired to a quern stone, where one-by-one they turned the stone anti-clockwise against him.[25] The sheaves were likely intended to represent the landlord, and their interment his death and burial. By turning the quern stone anti-clockwise the women

23 Ibid., 33.
24 Ibid., 30–1.
25 Ibid., 24.

symbolically worked to grind away his body. This is somewhat comparable to the practice of naming a corn dolly for an individual, and then burying it near the victim's home that they might rot with it.

The reference to Bridget conceivably relates to St. Brigid, who has a folkloric association with corn. Indeed, her symbol, the St. Brigid's Cross, is woven of corn, and the saint herself is sometimes represented by a corn dolly, which is laid in a straw-lined cradle known as 'Brigid's bed' during the observances of St. Brigid's feast day (1st February).

Another Irish curse involving the turning of stones is the custom attendant to bullaun ('bowl') stones. These are large flat rocks with one or more hemispherical depressions (*bullauns*) in their surface, whose basin-like hollows contain hefty stones proportionate in size to the cavity in which they sit. Although there are 837 bullaun stones recorded in Ireland's Sites and Monuments Record, many of these have lost their attendant stones. Of the stones surviving, some are marked with crosses, presumably to 'Christianise' them.

According to tradition, the loose stones are turned clockwise upon the bullaun as 'prayer stones', or anti-clockwise as 'cursing stones', which is done whilst naming the individual who is to receive the blessing or imprecation. The stone is thus revealed to be a source of neutral power, which is capable of being applied to dual ends—curse or cure. Whilst its benefic virtues are secured by turning the stone sunwise, its malefic powers are released through a widdershins or backwards turn (against the path of the sun), and thus against the natural order of things.

There is little agreement regarding the original purpose of bullauns, and considering their varying sizes, and the quantity of hollows they contain, they likely served a variety of purposes depending upon the people's needs. Accordingly, the uses and the beliefs regarding bullaun stones have conceivably evolved through the ages.

One suggestion is that bullauns were associated with a tradition of making hollows in front of burial tombs, which were filled with offerings of milk for the *Sídhe*. This custom is known of since at least the 19th Century, and some purport it to be a continuance of a pre-Christian practice. However, this theory is speculative at best, and most archaeologists believe bullauns actually date from the medieval period.

The majority of bullauns are in close proximity to ecclesiastical sites, which has caused many to posit a Christian origin for these stones. For example, there are several bullauns ('hollows') upon the face of the 2.5 metres square Keelers Stone, which is situated near the ruins of Kilmalkedar church, and in 1984 another bullaun stone with a single large hollow was unearthed nearby. This early Christian site, which is now associated with St. Brendan, was once the site of a 7th Century monastery founded by St. Maolcethair.

An association between bullaun stones and Christianity is also found in folklore. For example, bullauns with single depressions were oft-imagined to have been the pillows of saints, whilst paired hollows were fancied to have been formed by the knees of saints as they knelt in prayer.[26] Of course, such tales don't account for bullauns having seven, nine, or even fifteen hollows. Neither do they throw light upon why bullauns should have concomitant loose stones associated with them.

The belief bullaun hollows were formed by saints is illustrated by the legend of the 'Kneeling Stone' at St. Brigit's Shrine in Faughart (County Louth), whose paired hollows were supposedly formed when St. Brigit knelt upon the stone. This bullaun, along with others in its vicinity, serve as stations upon the St. Brigid's Shrine pilgrimage route. On arrival, the pilgrim announces their intent to undertake the pilgrimage by rubbing the first bullaun, after which they walk to the Kneeling Stone bullaun, where they kneel in prayer. Upon reaching the final bullaun the pilgrim uses waters collecting in its hollow to anoint the self with the sign of the cross, thereby symbolising their baptism into new life. Waters gathering in several of the bullauns at this site are renowned for having healing power.

Less saintly in origin are the twin indentations in a bullaun near the ruins of a medieval church at Myshall (County Carlow), which is sometimes called St. Brigit's Stone, ostensibly due to its proximity to a holy well dedicated to the saint. A legend attendant to this bullaun claims the depressions were made by the knees of a witch when she fell from the nearby Blackstairs Mountain. For this reason, the bullaun is known locally as 'the Witch's Stone'.

Some theorise the rounded stones found in bullaun hollows were left there by early Christian saints and missionaries, who carried consecrated stones on their journeys and placed them on un-hallowed altars

26 Peter Harbison, *Pilgrimage in Ireland: the Monuments and the People*, 1992, p. 223.

to sanctify them for the celebration of Mass. It has been suggested the stones were then left in situ to keep the faith alive amongst the local populace. These tokens of the faith may have been thought to embody the visiting saint's numinous power, which could be accessed in the saint's absence through magico-religious rites to procure blessing, healing, or cursing.[27]

The bullauns' hollows are assumed to have been formed by the constant devotional turning of these loose stones—clockwise for prayers and anti-clockwise for maledictions—which deed was carried out whilst making prayers to God and his saintly retinue. However, in similitude to other curses made at sanctified locales, through holy relics, and/or through invocation of heavenly powers, it was believed the malediction would rebound on the curser if made without just cause.

There is a 'curse stone' associated with an altar on the island of Caher (Ireland), where an ancient monastic site is situated. The stone rests on the altar of a ruined church, and to access its power the individual had to fast and pray before turning the stone anti-clockwise. If the malediction was successful a storm would arise and the cursed one would be destroyed.

Another altar stone serving as a bullaun is situated within an enclosure at the centre of Inishmurray. This holy island, just off the Sligo coast, was a place of pilgrimage, and the enclosure, which once constituted an ancient monastic settlement, contains beehive cells, churches, carved stones, and grave slabs. Sitting on the large altar stone are a number of hefty stones known as the *Clocha Breacha* ('cursing' or 'speckled stones'), which were turned three times by pilgrims to secure their desire—clockwise for blessings and healing, or anti-clockwise for maledictions. A variation of the Inishmurray curse rite was to circle the 'Altar of Cursing' three or nine times whilst saying the correct imprecatory prayer, and turning a curse stone with each pass of the altar. As with other maledictions empowered by holy agency, unjust curses would rebound on the invocator.

The 'speckled stones' of Inishmurray are reputed to have great power. One early 19th Century tale tells how the islanders turned the stones widdershins to deliver 'natural justice' upon some men connected with

27 William Stokes, *The Life and Labours in Art and Archaeology of George Petrie*, p. 296.

the coastguard who had angered them, and the men died at sea soon after. It is also said a woman once made pilgrimage to the stones to lay a curse on Hitler.

Cursing stones are also found at an ecclesiastical site at Killinagh, which comprises of a ruined church and holy well, both dedicated to St. Brigid, a mound (thought to be a derelict megalithic tomb) known as the Queen's Grave or St. Brigid's House, and a large bullaun known as St. Brigid's cursing stone.[28] Upon the face of this stone slab are several depressions varying from 15 to 30 cm. in width, and nestled in each is a rounded stone perfectly fitting its hollow. According to local lore a curse could be put upon a victim by turning the stones anti-clockwise in the morning, but if the intent was unjust the imprecatory power would rebound upon the stone-turner before nightfall.

When William Wakeman investigated the Killinagh site in 1875 a local said it was customary 'when any of the neighbours had a grudge against a real or supposed enemy, and wished him harm, [they would] proceed to the 'altar' and anathematise him.[29] This suggests the 'just' and 'fair' curses laid by the stones were considered analogous to the rite of excommunication, which is to say the maledictions secured were intended to punish those who were 'ungodly' or had transgressed God's law.

Another rite associated with the Killinagh cursing stones is related in an 1894 edition of *Folklore*:

> [St. Brigid's Altar] is a large horizontal slab, with twelve or thirteen bullauns or basins cut in it, and in each bullaun, save one, there is a large round stone. The curser takes up one of the stones and places it in the empty basin-and so on, one after another, till all have been gone over. During the movement he is cursing his enemy, and if he removes all the stones without letting any one of them slip (no easy

28 According to local legend, a stone standing in Drumcoo (County Fermanagh) originally stood next to the Killinagh cursing stones. It is marked with a figure variously interpreted as being St. Patrick, a druid, or the 'pagan god' *Crom Crúaich* —meaning 'crooked one—and for this reason a nearby street is named *Crom Crúaich Way*.

29 'On the Bullàn, or Rock-Basin, as Found in Ireland; With Special Reference to Two Inscribed Examples' by W. F. Wakeman, *Proceedings of the Royal Irish Academy* 1 (1889–91), p. 262.

> operation, on account of their form), his curses will have effect, but not otherwise. If he lets one slip, the curses will return on his own head.[30]

A cursing tradition is also attendant to the bullaun on the three-mile long pilgrimage route at Glencolumcille (County Donegal), which pilgrimage is traditionally made in honour of Colm Cille on his Saint's day (9th June). The bullaun is sited next to a cairn, and on its large flat surface sits a rounded 'prayer stone' serving as an instrument of curing and cursing. The stone's twain power ostensibly derives from its association with St. Colmcille, who was renowned both for his blessings and his many formidable curses.

To access the stone's power, the pilgrim had first to make three circuits of the cairn, all the while saying three Paternosters, three Hail Mary's, three Gloria's, and the Creed. This ritualistic act served to purify, prepare, and sanctify the pilgrim before they made their entreaty, and is analogous to the purifications undertaken by ceremonial magicians before making conjurations. After the prayer for effect, the pilgrim passes the rounded stone thrice about his or her body whilst saying, "In the name of the Father, the Son, and the Holy Ghost," a binding phrase which marks the prayer's completion. There were once three stones on the Glencolumcille bullaun slab, which were likely conceived to represent this Holy Trinity, the sacred powers invoked to grant the pilgrim's desire. Another station on the Glencolumbkille pilgrimage is the 'Flagstone of the Request', which flat boulder is marked with a circled cross. Should the pilgrim walk thrice around this boulder in prayer and then jump off, their request would be granted.

Perhaps the most infamous bullauns are those on Tory Island, which was allegedly the stronghold of the Fomorians, and home to their king, Balor of the Evil Eye. During the 6th Century, St. Colmcille also established a monastery there. One imprecatory bullaun, which probably started life as a holy water receptacle, is found near the entrance of the ruined Church of the Seven, where the corpses of seven people who died of a shipwreck are buried. The Edinburgh naturalist James Spence

30 'Cursing Stones in Counties Fermanagh, Cavan, etc' by G. H. Kinahan, *Folklore*, Volume 5, Number 1, 1894, pp. 3–4.

wrote how curses could be laid at one of the Tory Island bullauns by turning the stone in the hollow whilst repeating the victim's name, which secured their death within the year.[31]

The most notorious of all the Tory Island bullauns is the *Cloch na Mallacht* ('the Cursing Stone'), which is situated at the island's northern end. The *Cloch na Mallacht* is one of the stations of the *An Turas Mor*, which is a clockwise pilgrimage route around the island's holy sites. However, if one wished to curse an enemy, this pilgrimage route was instead traversed in a reverse direction, and at the culmination of this adverse perambulation the would-be curser turned the prayer stone upside down, which binding act served to seal the rite.

In encircling the holy acre contrary to the normal deosil (sun-wise) route, those walking the backwards path trod against the sun and the natural order of things. In so doing they evoked powers oppositional to those of light, life, and growth, which facilitated their rite of death, darkness, and decay. As the widdershins route was a perversion of the proper practice, this backwards pilgrimage also had the potential to rile the saint in the manner of a *clamour*. Analogous is 'the reverse journey', where the would-be curser went to a church and visited the Stations of the Cross in reverse order whilst praying for their enemy's downfall.

Of all the curses unleashed at Tory Island, the most notorious concerns HMS Wasp. On 21st September 1884, bailiffs set sail in HMS Wasp with the intent of evicting islanders who hadn't paid their rent, but during the early hours of the 22nd September the ship ran aground on the rocks surrounding Tory Island, even though the experienced crew were familiar with the journey. The wrecked ship quickly sank, and of the fifty-eight crewmen, only six survived. A member of the Heggarty family, who was then serving as 'King of Tory', claimed to have caused the tragedy by turning the curse stones. As a result, the parish priest, Father O'Donnel, took the cursing stones from the bullaun and threw them from the cliff overlooking the wreck of the HMS Wasp. The 'King of Tory' is an ancient office allegedly held by pre-historic figures including the Fomorian kings Conand and Balor of the Evil Eye, and is a tradition still kept to this day.

31 *Transactions of the Edinburgh Field Naturalists and Microscopial Society 1902–1907.*

In addition to the *Cloch na Mallacht*, Tory Island has a wonder-working stone in the form of an ancient Tau-Cross, which locals pray before for saintly intercession. Because the relic stands beside the harbour it is much resorted to by fishermen. The cross is carved from a slab of mica slate, and as mica is not found on the island the relic is presumed to have been brought to Tory Island during the 12th Century as a gift for the island's monastery. However, despite its Christian reputation, the stone has a darker aspect, and in *The Nature of Things*, the anthropologist Lyall Watson writes how it:

> ...serves the islanders as a secret weapon. When threatened they gather on the cliffs and point in the direction of marauders, tax-gatherers, and other forms of piracy. And, they say, it never fails to spell disaster for an invader.[32]

Like other holy objects used for cursing, it was only deemed acceptable to use the Tau Cross for imprecatory purposes when the cause was just, for example, the obtainment of 'natural justice' against sinners, such as pirates and marauders.

On the Isle of Man, the imprecatory use of bullauns is associated with a potent Manx curse known as the *Shiaght mynney mollaght*, meaning 'the seven swearings of a curse'. In his 1939 work, 'Sorcery and Witchcraft in Mann', D. Craine writes how the curse is exacted using a round 'swearing stone', which sits in a cup-shaped hollow on a larger rock. The stone is turned in its hollow seven times in a widdershins direction, almost as if grinding the victim away. According to tradition, this rite was worked by night upon the summit of Tynwald Hill, or elsewise on its north side, north being a direction associated in folklore with darkness and the Devil.

A comparable rite was worked using a stone at the ruins of a keeill (early Christian chapel) in Raby (Isle of Man). The stone is a large circular mass of granite, about a metre wide and almost as deep, with a round cup-like cavity in its centre, which is about three inches deep. It is marked on the 1869 Ordinance Survey as a font, and Oswald's *Vestigia Insulae Manniae Antiquiora* (1860) describes it as an 'ancient baptismal

32 Lyall Watson, *The Nature of Things; The Secret Life of Inanimate Objects*, p. 35.

font—a rude granite block', which stood three yards from a holy well that was 'once reputed to be curative.' The interpretation of the stone as a font is perhaps commended by its proximity to the holy well, whose waters might have been used to fill it. However, some archaeologists believe the stone may have been a base for a cross rather than a font, or perhaps a hollow in which corn was ground, especially as the latter are found at other Manx keeills.

Whatever the stone's original purpose, with the passing of time the stone gained a darker reputation, as attested by this entry in *A Vocabulary of the Anglo Manx Dialect* (1924):

> *CURSING STONE.* Near the old Keeill at Reaby on the top of the houghs of Magher n Ruilhck ('field of the graveyard') is a large round stone raised on an artificial mound. In the centre of the stone is a circular hollow such as those in which the old Celt, when he wished ill to an enemy, twisted his thumb round against the sun and cursed him with a 'prayer of cursing'.

The rite as described above is somewhat comparable to the practice of aiding wish-fulfilment by circling a hagstone with the thumb, which is traced deosil for blessings and widdershins for cursing.

Noting their association with ecclesiastical sites, some theorise bullauns were once used to dispense holy water, especially as many are situated on pilgrim routes. Moreover, the rainwaters collecting in bullaun basins are often ascribed similar curative and apotropaic powers as holy water. This is exemplified by the beliefs attendant to the bullaun atop a megalithic burial mound in Ballyvourney (County Cork). Rainwaters collecting in this bullaun, and earth taken from the mound, were both used for healing, and clouties were attached to the bushes around the mound.[33] This bullaun is also a station on the *turas* of St. Gobnait, which ritual pilgrimage was carried out at the Ballyvourney monastic site. Other stations on the Ballyvourney *turas* include a large slab next to the bullaun, known as St. Gobnait's Grave, and a Sheela-na-Gig set

33 W. G. Wood-Martin, *Traces of the Elder Faiths of Ireland* (Vol. 1), 1902, p. 323.

inside a nearby church ruin, which figure is imagined to be a depiction of St. Gobnait, and which the pilgrim is to reach in and rub.

Another curative bullaun with close proximity to a holy well is found at the monastic site of Clonmacnoise (Offaly). This bullaun was long visited by pilgrims seeking its waters for healing warts and cattle diseases. The stone's curative powers ostensibly derive from its proximity to the holy well, and its positioning on a sanctified site. A comparable pairing is found at the early ecclesiastical settlement of Lemanaghan (County Offaly), where there is a bullaun with a large single hollow next to a holy well that is dedicated to the settlement's founder, St. Manchan. On the anniversary of St. Manchan's death, pilgrims wishing to be cured of blindness, lameness and other chronic disorders would visit the well and tie clouties upon the nearby rag tree.[34]

Another bullaun whose waters possess curative power is the 'Deer Stone', which sits within the ruins of the Glendalough monastic site (County Wicklow). Its name commemorates a legend about a wild doe, which came down and filled the bullaun with milk after St. Kevin prayed for milk to save the lives of two orphaned babies. In serving as the locus of a saintly miracle, the stone was sanctified, and the rainwaters gathering there were thereafter accorded great curative power. This power was secured by making pilgrimage to the stone before sunrise on the Sunday, Tuesday, and Thursday of the same week, and on each visit the pilgrim was to crawl seven times about the stone on their knees, which was done whilst fasting and saying the necessary prayers. The supplicatory act of crawling about on all fours whilst uttering pleas for saintly intercession is somewhat concordant to the act of clamouring.

In considering these exemplars, it is revealed how the power accorded to bullaun water is bound up with sanctity of place. This is also intimated by the healing virtue ascribed to waters collecting in other stony basins at holy sites, whether wrought by hand of man or nature. Implicit is the idea waters become sanctified when collecting in stones

34 Crushed iron ore was found in the vicinity of the Lemanaghan bullaun, which has caused some to suggest it was used to crush and sort ore for metallurgy. Lending weight to this hypothesis is the existence of a bullaun stone in the ironworking area of nearby Gallen Priory (County Offaly), which likewise has a single large basin worn into it. Others theorise single basin bullauns might have been used to grind small quantities of grain or herbs for sacred rites.

considered to be holy, whether because the stone had an earlier (real or imagined) sacred function or because of its positioning in a sacred site. For example, the rainwaters collecting in the ancient holy water font in the sacristy of Timoleague Friary were believed to cure warts when the afflicted fingers were dipped into its waters, for which reason it became known as the 'Wart Well.' Wart charming is also associated with a bullaun at Parc-y-Ceryg Sanctaidd ('The Field of the Holy Stones') in Llanddowror (Carmarthenshire, Wales). In latter years, the site was on a funeral path, and when coffins were carried through it on their way to the churchyard they were momentarily laid upon a large square stone, which was carved with a cross. After the paternoster was said, the coffin was sprinkled with holy water using a cup, which was taken from an adjacent large square stone with a basin worn into it. The waters collecting within this basin were sought for a wart cure, which was effected by casting pins into the water, ostensibly to charge them with curative power, and then taking them out to prick the warts.[35] It has been suggested 'The Field of the Holy Stones' was once a field-altar akin to medieval Irish examples, and the hollow was used as a bullaun for rites of blessing and cursing.

Throughout Britain and Ireland, curative holy powers have also been ascribed to waters gathering in the empty sockets of foundation stones once holding crosses in place. Illustrative is the old Cornish custom of using waters collecting in such cavities to baptise dolls for the purposes of magical protection, with a pin afterwards being dropped in the waters as a votive, which practice is attendant to other holy wells. Curative powers were also ascribed to waters collecting in the cavity of an ancient stone cross base in the corner of a churchyard in Old Donagh (County Monaghan). Because these waters reputedly healed warts it is locally known as the 'Warty Well.'

At the medieval ecclesiastical site of Old Leighlin (County Carlow) there is a holy well that allegedly sprung from the base of a stone cross, and in the grounds of the adjacent medieval cathedral is a bullaun stone. The holy well is dedicated to St. Laserian—also known as St. Molasog's, St. Molasha's, or St. Molaise's Well—and is an age-old site of pilgrimage and veneration due to its power to effect great miracles. To this day visi-

35 Mary Curtis, *Antiquities of Laugharne*, p. 214.

tors still leave votive offerings for saintly intercession, and afterwards tie cloutie rags to a nearby tree. On St. Laserian's Feast Day (18th April) pilgrims visit the well after Mass to say prayers and drink from its waters. However, the well has a darker side, and those undertaking false oaths before it would suffer a great judgement, and would be cursed.

The hallowed waters of St. Laserian's well are not alone in having capacity to curse and cure, as proven by the long tradition of making visitation to holy wells for boons as diverse as healing, wish-fulfilment, romance, natural justice, and the cursing of enemies. Implicit is the idea that power is power, and can be diverted to an array of ends, which in and of themselves have no moral value. Indeed, any value placed upon these desires, such as 'good' or 'evil, are subjective individual judgements based upon the vagaries of one's own personal moral compass, rather than universal truths, and as such vary between individuals, time, and place. However, in similitude to other curses laid by saintly intercession, it was sometimes believed unjust or undeserved curses would rebound upon the operant.

To access a holy well's power, it is traditional to undertake a rite known as a 'round'. This typically involves walking about the well in a sun-wise direction whilst saying prayers to invoke the saint's power. The pilgrim then drinks or bathes in the well's waters, and makes a votive offering of a coin or similar to the spirit of the water, (the saint). Finally, a rag or cloutie is tied to a nearby tree. Yet, if the pilgrim desired to curse a wrongdoer, they would instead walk widdershins about the well, whilst praying against the victim, all the while hoping the spirit or Saint of the well would recognise the injustice suffered and grant their desire for retribution. Herein is demonstrated how the one saintly power can be directed to dual-purposes through twain expressions of the one rite.

The ability of certain holy wells to grant wishes both fair and foul is demonstrated by a number of regional folk customs. For example, at Ffynnon Gegidog ('St. George's Well') in Denbigshire, waters from the well could bestow curative blessings when sprinkled over man or beast whilst saying the prayer, 'Rhad Duw a Sant Sior arnat' ('the blessing of God and St. George be on thee'). Afterwards a coin was placed in the

Poor Box. However, the same waters were also accorded a power for evil, and could be used to lay curses.[36]

A similar dual power was ascribed to Ffynnon Dwynwen (Anglesey), whose waters could be used to heal sick animals and to pronounce curses. Likewise, St. Cybi's Well near Holyhead (Anglesey) was visited for healing and divination, and also cursing. These curses were exacted by writing the victim's name on paper, which was then hidden under one of the well's banks.

At Llanllawer Holy Well (also known as Ffynnon Gapan, Pembrokeshire), the waters were renowned for their miraculous healing properties, especially in the curing of eye problems. This blessing was obtained by dropping straight pins or coins into the well as a votive offering, whilst curses were made by casting 'evil crooked pins' into the water. Herein the twain manifestations of the pin become as fetishes of the straight and crooked powers, namely the creative and blessed power of the 'straight' pin and the destructive and accursed power of the 'crooked' pin. At Ffynnon y Gaer (near Dolgellau, Merioneth), pins were also dropped into the water in exchange for the cursing and bewitchment of enemies, although no mention is made as to whether or not these pins were bent.

A darker rite undertaken at holy wells was described by the archaeologist Ralph Merrifield, who wrote how frogs representing the victim were struck with pins and cast into the well's depths. The one casting the curse then trod the path against the sun whilst muttering baleful curses, thereby drawing down dark powers upon the victim.[37] A comparable procedure was observed until the early 20th Century at Ffynnon Parc Mawr (Anglesey), which holy well was also known as Ffynnon Goch ('The Red Well'), ostensibly on account of its chalybeate waters, and like other iron-rich wells it also had a reputation for healing. The following account explicates the rubric by which curses were made at this well:

> Not long ago a man found a frog stuck full of pins or needles in this well. The ceremonial was to stick pins in a frog,

36 Francis Jones, *The Holy Wells of Wales*, pp. 106–7, 118.

37 Ibid., 155.

> place it between two stones and deposit it in a well with a piece of slate on which the name of the person to be bewitched was scratched: sometimes the heart of a black cat was added.[38]

Whilst this rite is suggestive of witchcraft, the use of proxies for cursing is not alien to 'Christian' magic, as evidenced by numerous accounts of clergy and lay people baptising and saying masses over poppets in order to consecrate and empower them. It is thus possible the aforementioned execration was intended to be effectuated by a vengeful saint rather than a demonic power, as was the custom at other curse wells.

Another cursing rite expedited by means of batrachian effigy was observed at the nearby well of Ffynnon Eilian (Llaneilian, Anglesey). Here a live frog was run through with a skewer, after which corks were placed at either end of the spike. The impaled frog was then left to float in the well, the victim suffering for as long as the tormented creature remained alive upon its dark waters. Herein the frog became a living effigy of the intended victim, with the curse obtaining its nefarious effect by means of the well's power, which was derived from its saintly dedication.

Frogs and toads were commonly used as proxies in curse rites, ostensibly due to their fancied resemblance to the human form. For example, in 1871 a black Buckley earthenware pipkin containing a nail-struck frog was found by a labourer when removing an earthen bank on Penrhos Bardwyn farm (Holyhead, Anglesey). The pipkin's opening was covered by a slate, which was etched on both sides with the victim's name, 'Nanney Roberts.' This assemblage, which combines a batrachian effigy with a slate scratched with the victim's initials, is now housed in the Gwynedd Museum and Art Gallery (Bangor).

Interestingly, during the same century a Welsh gypsy named Bob visited a local cunning man to seek revenge on a man named Will Solomon, who had run off with his wife. The cunning man advised Bob to:

38 E Neil Baynes, 'Anglesey Folklore'. *Proceedings of the Anglesey Antiquarian Society* (1928) p. 83.

> ...buy a pennyworth of new pins, then to find a toad, and stick all the pins in its back and belly, till it looked like a hedgehog...[then] dig a hole at the foot of a grave where one of Will Solomon's kinsfolk was buried, and there at midnight...bury a cup with the toad covered up in it by a piece of slate.

At midnight in five weeks time he was to dig up the cup containing the toad, which would cause Will Solomon to be driven mad. However, Bob buried the frog in the wrong grave, and did not raise the cup at midnight as instructed. This caused the spell to backfire, and as a result Bob himself was driven mad, and later died in Caernarvon.[39]

At Ffynnon Elian (Llaneilian) curses were not only exacted by frogs, but also by wax effigies. Illustrative is a bundle uncovered from the well's north facing wall, which consisted of a crude wax effigy pinned through its middle to a small piece of slate (two by three inches). The left arm of the doll had been broken off and the slate was etched with an oblong marked at the centre with the initials 'R.F.' (presumably those of the victim), with its four corners marked with the letters 'OAM', 'MEM', 'AGM' and '—M'.

Slate is commonly used in cursing rites around Anglesey, its grey 'leaden' colour evoking the same cold and saturnine powers as its metallurgic cousin.[40] The pairing of slate and effigy is also reminiscent of the Græco-Roman practice of coupling *defixiones* (curse tablets) with *kolossoi* (effigies), which assemblages were often deposited in water, even as curse slates were consigned to the depths of holy wells. Concordant is the placement of written petitionary prayers in wells and bodies of water so as to procure the indwelling saint or spirit's aid.

A simpler and more popular method of cursing at Ffynnon Eilian was to throw a cork into the well, which served as a proxy of the victim. These corks were presumably etched with the victim's initials, even as initials were scratched into the pebbles and slates cast into other cursing wells.

39 Francis Hindes Groome, *In Gipsy Tents*, 1880.
40 Merrifield, *The Archaeology of Ritual and Magic*, p. 155.

St. Eilian was a 6th Century Saint who was sent to Anglesey by the Pope, and thereafter lived in the north of the island as a hermit. On his feast day (13th January), pilgrims visited St. Eilian's well in Llaneilian to drink of its waters and kneel before an altar in the small chapel (6 metres by 4 metres) housing it. These waters were much visited for the healing of the sick, and those seeking its curative powers would typically bathe in its waters. The well was also repaired to for the blessing of livestock and corn.

To 'pay' for the Saint's intercession, pilgrims would afterwards retire to the nearby Church of St. Eilian, where their monetary offerings were placed into an old oak chest called 'Cyff Eilian', which had the date '1667' picked out on the lid in nail heads. These monies were used to help maintain the Saint's church and shrine. However, the trunk had a more sinister reputation, and could also be used for cursing, as attested by this account from 1802:

> '...the country people are said to drop a piece of money [through a small slit in the lid], uttering their maledictions against their enemies. The black gentleman is thus fed to work evil against the offender. This uncharitable and unchristian custom, if true, seems almost too bad even for monkish times, much worse to be continued now.'[41]

Due to its dual-power to curse and cure, Ffynnon Eilian became known as 'the witching well', and some alleged a witch's craggy face could be seen in the rock face from which the waters flow.

At Llandrillo-yn-Rhos (Conwy) there is another Ffynnon Elian (St. Elian's Well), which was equally notorious for its maledictive power. According to legend, its waters sprung up during the 6th Century when the travelling St. Elian prayed for water to quench his thirst. Thankful for this miracle, the Saint prayed the spring might forever slake the wishes of those visiting it. Thereafter it was much resorted to as a wishing and healing well, with clouties sometimes being tied to nearby trees. However, the wishes granted at Ffynnon Elian were not always benefic

41 J. Skinner, 'A Ten Days Tour Through the Isle of Anglesey, December 1802.' *Archaelogia Cambrensis Supplement,* pp. 60–61.

in nature, and during the 18th Century it began to acquire a reputation as a powerful cursing well. Interestingly, an alternative tradition claims the well sprung up when St. Elian thrust his sword into the earth, which aggressive and penetrative motif is evocative of the well's power to 'wound'.

The earliest reference to Ffynnon Elian (Conwy) as a locus for procuring natural justice is found in a report carried out in 1775 by the Revd. John Lloyd of Caerwys for inclusion in Thomas Pennant's *A Tour in Wales*, and speaks of the well's three-fold power:

> This well has been formerly much resorted to, and is still in some degree by those who labour under any infirmity of mind or body; who after invoking the saint of the place if they happen to recover, attribute it entirely to his gracious interposition.
>
> Others repair hither to curse their neighbours or others who may have obliged them, and to pray that sudden death or some dreadful calamity may not fail to overtake them. By offering up their devotions at the well and depositing some money in the poor's box in Llanelian church, they make no doubt of obtaining their requests, be they ever so unreasonable.
>
> Others again who had been robbed of their property have repaired hither and prayed to St. Elian that he would discover to them the thief, and enable them to recover what had been stolen from them.

From this it can be seen the well was visited for curing, cursing, and the recovery of stolen goods. Illustrative of the latter is a tale about a stolen coverlet, which was collected by the Revd. John Lloyd during his 1775 survey. The incident concerns a woman from Llandegla who, with a friend in tow, made the forty-mile trip to Ffynnon Elian in order to ask St. Elian to reveal who had stolen her coverlet, and to ask for its return. On this journey the women passed a number of other holy wells, which suggests Ffynnon Elian's reputation surpassed that of its neighbouring wells.

After visiting Ffynnon Elian and offering up prayers there, the two women repaired to the nearby church of Llanelian, where they placed their votive offering of coins into the poor box dedicated to the Saint's memory. The woman whose coverlet had been stolen then knelt in prayer before the altar, and asked St. Elian that he might discover the thief and restore her coverlet to her. With this entreaty complete, the woman got up and waited for her friend to finish her devotions. After much time had passed the woman asked her friend why she continued to kneel for so long. The kneeling woman confessed she herself had stolen the coverlet, and found herself stuck to the spot by St. Elian's power. Moreover, she feared she would be stuck there forever unless her larcenous deed was forgiven. Pitying the poor penitent, the woman forgave her friend, which immediately restored the use of her limbs.

When Pennant eventually published Revd. John Lloyd's report in his *A Tour of Wales*, he affirmed both curse and cure alike were obtained through St. Eilian's intercession, and gave his own personal experiences of the holy well:

> The well of St. Elian...has been in great repute for the cures of all diseases, by means of the intercession of the saint who was first invoked by earnest prayers in the neighbouring church. He was also applied to on less worthy occasions, and made the instrument of discovering thieves, and of recovering stolen goods. Some repair to him to imprecate their neighbours and to request the saint to afflict with sudden death, or with some great misfortune, any persons who may have offended them. The belief in this is still strong; for three years have not passed since I was threatened by a fellow (who imagined I had injured him) with the vengeance of St. Elian, and a journey to the well to curse me with effect.[42]

42 Pennant, *Tours in Wales*, Volume 3, p. 158.

At Ffynnon Eilian (Conwy) the rites were presided over by a human 'well guardian'. The first known guardian was Margaret Holland, who was the estranged wife of the Revd. Jeoffrey Holland, and lived nearby at Cefn-y-Ffynnon farm. Margaret served in the capacity of 'priestess of the well' from the end of the 18th Century through to her death in 1810. After Margaret's death the farm was let to farmer Robert Jones and his wife, and with it they inherited the role of 'guardians of the well'.

Somewhen in the early 1820s the Jones' family moved away, and the well's guardianship was taken over by John Evans, who became known as Jac Ffynnon Elian. During his teenage years, Evans had served as a tailor's apprentice in the nearby parish of Llandrillo-yn-Rhos, and at that time was familiar with both the well and the 'priestess', Margaret Holland. Evans served as *offeiriad* ('priest') for about twenty years, until his conversion to the Baptist faith somewhen between the late 1840s and early 1850s, and was the last person to serve the role. After his conversion, and with the help of a printer and fellow Baptist from Anglesey, he wrote a book about his tenure entitled *Llyfr Ffynnon Elian* ('The Book of Ffynnon Elian'). Much to the delight of local churches, once Evans had relinquished his role, the well was dismantled. However, this did not destroy its reputation, and even in the 1860s, a visitor to the remains of Ffynnon Elian, 'noticed corks and pins stuck in them, floating in the well.' Tales of the well's power to curse were also recounted beyond the 19th Century, and the rites used to adjure the presiding Saint to injure one's enemies were collected by folklorists and published in guidebooks to the region, which conceivably served as instruction to those who were more than idly curious.

For the service of laying and lifting curses at Ffynnon Eilian (Conwy), the well guardians charged a not inconsiderable sum, part of which payment was thrown directly into the well as an offering. By 1820, the cost to lay a curse had risen from one to five shillings, whilst the cost to lift a curse had jumped from ten to fifteen shillings.

Before laying a curse, the well-guardian recorded the victim's name in a book, and although a proxy of the victim was always used, the method varied, which is to say the imprecatory rite was governed by the well-guardian's ingenium rather than any specific ritual formula. The rites themselves typically involved the use of Psalms, biblical passages, and excerpts taken from the Apocrypha, which reinforced the idea the curse was worked through holy power and saintly intercession rather than diabolic agency. In the eyes of the Christian populace who flocked to the well, this conferred a semblance of legitimacy upon the rites, regardless of the church's condemnation of such practices. Moreover, many believed curses were only effective at Ffynnon Eilian when the victim 'deserved' it, and this is attested by the many petitions made at the well to avenge adulterers, thieves, traitors, and other 'sinners'.

The proxy used by the well-guardian could take many forms. One method was to scratch the victim's initials onto a pebble or slate using a nail, or to write the initials on a piece of paper, which was then folded in lead and tied to a piece of slate, thereby magically linking the object with the victim. This proxy was then cast into the well as the curse was pronounced, with a small quantity of the water being raised up and thrown back.

An alternative method was to throw a pin or cork into the waters as the victim was named, or to fix a pin through the name in the well-guardian's book. Several visitors to the well recalled seeing pin-struck corks floating upon the surface of the well, which were thought to be curses; the cork ostensibly represented the victim and the pin the curse struck into them, thereby evoking the motif of the pin-struck poppet.

On occasion the well-guardian used an effigy of wax, clay, or dough, which was pierced whilst speaking secret curses. The transfixed doll was then dipped thrice into the well's accursed waters, and after this black baptism was consigned to the depths forever. One woman, who suspected her husband of adultery, fashioned a figure of clay in his likeness, struck its heart with pins, and cast it into Ffynnon Elian, which caused him to suffer terrible heart troubles. A week later she revisited the well, took the effigy out of the waters, and put the pins in the head and elsewhere, which caused her husband to suffer pain in the corresponding members. After several weeks of torture, her husband felt pangs of guilt for his adultery and repented his wayward behaviour, which his wife forgave.

Another curse exacted by effigy concerns a man desiring to gain natural justice on his cruel and unjust uncle. To achieve this, he made a wax image in his uncle's likeness, struck it with pins, and tied it to a lump of copper, which assemblage he dangled over Ffynnon Elian on a piece of cord. As he lowered the wax figure into the well, he uttered 'secret words of cursing', expressing his wish that the uncle might suffer continual pain and lose money, property, and possessions. Thrice he plunged the figure into the waters, and on the third time he let it sink to the bottom, where it was left for the waters to do their work. After suffering constant severe pain, a burglary, and a fire that burnt some of his property to the ground, the cruel uncle paid his nephew to lift the curse.

A particularly detailed account of an imprecatory ceremony carried out at Fynnon Eilian is given in Lewis's *Topographical Dictionary of Wales* (1833):

> Fynnon Eilian, which, even in the present age, is annually visited by hundreds of people, for the reprehensible purpose of invoking curses upon the heads of those who have grievously offended them. The ceremony is performed by the applicant standing upon a certain spot near the well, whilst the owner of it reads a few passages of the sacred scriptures, and then, taking a small quantity of water, gives it to the former to drink, and throws the residue over his head, which is repeated three times, the party continuing to mutter imprecations in whatever terms his vengeance may dictate.

Notably, it was the supplicant, and not the well-guardian, who muttered the imprecations, and these took the form of an extemporised outpouring of hatred, rather than conforming to a formulaic charm. This implies the guardian's role was to ritually facilitate the curse rather than invoke it, for which reason unjust curses rebounded on the supplicant rather than the well-guardian.

Well water from Fynnon Eilian was sometimes taken home for use against enemies, and there is a record of one Breconshire farmer taking away two small barrels of water for such purposes. However, when fetching water from the barrels to throw after an enemy, the barrels burst and the water splashed him, which bewitched him forever after.

When it came to lifting curses, the well-guardian brought a variety of counter-charms into play, including mysterious Latin incantations, the reciting of psalms and biblical passages, treading three circles about the well, pouring water from the well over the petitioner's head, and the retrieval and destruction of the proxy. Afterwards, the well waters were typically checked to see whether they 'sparkled' or not, which omen served to reveal whether the curse had been successfully lifted.

Where the proxy took the form of a slate tablet inscribed with the victim's initials, this was removed, ground into dust, mixed with salt, and burned upon a fire. The cursed individual also had to drink some of the well's water at home, which counter-charm was reinforced by reading aloud portions of the *Book of Job* and *Psalm* 38 on three successive Fridays.[43] *Psalm* 38 is a prayer of contrition.

It was believed those who had been 'put into the well' became increasingly ill, and/or met with misfortune, 'every new moon.' Several accounts also allude to the curse-lifting rite being timed by the moon, which suggests a link between the lunar phases and the well-water's power. For example, on one occasion the 'priestess' Margaret Holland lifted a curse by taking three lots of water from the well on the night of the new moon, and on three successive Fridays a glass of the well-water was drunk whilst reading select verses from the Psalms.

On another occasion, a man wishing to be released from the suffering caused by St. Elian's curse was told the proper time to be 'pulled out of the well' was the full moon, and until then he was to read a number of Psalms to stave off the well's deleterious effect. When the night of the full moon came round he had to repeat the Lord's Prayer and throw all the water out of the well. Then, once the well had refilled, he filled a cup with its water, drank some, and threw the remainder over his head. With this done, he reached into the well and retrieved the accursed assemblage, which comprised of a slate, a cork, and a sheet of lead bound with wire. Inside the lead was a piece of paper marked with his initials and some crosses.

Tales abound of the terrible effects suffered by those consigned to the depths of Ffynnon Eilian's dark waters, and it was said:

> Such persons cannot prosper either in body or estate, but must endure bodily pain, and be unsuccessful in his worldly affairs, until his name be taken out of the well

43 Jones, *The Holy Wells of Wales*, pp. 119–123.

> [i.e., until the slate, pebble or paper etched with their initials were removed].[44]

One woman from Dolanog (Montgomery) became bedridden after being 'put in the well', and only regained her ability to walk many years later when the one who cursed her died. A Non-conformist minister also became seriously ill after being 'offered' up to the well.

Another of the well's victims was a man from Montgomery, who was cursed at Ffynnon Eilian after a love affair during his youth. When the man asked the well-guardian how the curse could be counteracted, he was told it could not affect him if he remained within the bounds of his own property. The man therefore spent the remainder of his days as a bachelor, and never left his house until the day he died, when his lifeless corpse was carried to the church. Such is testament to the very real fear people had of the well's power.

In Angharad Llwyd's 'History of the Island of Mono or Anglesey' (1833), an account is given of a bed-ridden woman who believed her affliction was caused by a vengeful neighbour making an offering at Ffynnon Eilian (Conwy). She speedily recovered when her husband countered the curse by 'taking her name out of the well, at the expense of 2s.6d.'

Animals were also victim of the well's power. For example, when a dog's name was put in the well the poor animal was run over shortly thereafter, and when a pig was similarly cursed it had disastrous results for the farmer.

In the 19th Century, Fynnon Eilian was the subject of a poem by the Welsh poet Charlotte Wardle, which was published in 1814 under the title, *St. Elian's* or the *Cursing Well*. The poem is a lengthy tale of rivalry, jealousy, and revenge, and evocatively describes the ominous atmosphere about the titular well:

> *Not in the mystic Elian's grove,*
> *Did feather'd songsters sing of love,*
> *But birds of omen harbour'd there,*
> *And fill'd with brooding shrieks the air;*

44 *The Edinburgh Magazine and Literary Miscellany* (Volume 83).

The blasted trees so rent and riven,
By fi'ry speed of burning levin,
Had prov'd the bolt and wrath o heaven,
Some stretch their wither'd arms on high,
In scornful mood to mock the sky,
Whilst shadow'd by their branches sear,
And deep, and dark, and dank and drear,
The baneful fountain rises here.

Wardle's poem is faithful to the practices typically associated with Ffynnon Eilian, which suggests she was familiar with the well's customs. In her poem, Wardle re-imagines the 'well guardian' or 'priestess' as an old witch, who places a curse on behalf of the villain of the piece. Yet, even here, the curse is exacted by invocation of the saint, reflecting the belief that wishes to harm or heal were made at the well by St. Elian's holy intercession, and not through witchcraft or the devil:

The witch drew water from the well—
Invok'd the saint, and forthwith sped
Beneath the wave the mystic lead
On which Sir Gryfydd's name was read;
The charm has pass'd her quiv'ring lips,
And now once more the bowl she dips,
Beneath the darkling surface—then
Repeats her orgies o'er again.

However, not all wishes made at holy wells were granted by virtue of saints, and at several cursing wells the presiding spirit was syncretised with infernal entities. Illustrative is the Devil's Whispering Well, which is located in the churchyard wall at Bishop's Lydeard (Somerset), and by whispering the names of one's enemies into its dark waters a terrible curse could be invoked upon the named parties.

It is possible the likes of Ffynnon y Cythraul ('Devil's Well') in Caernarvonshire, Ffynnon Pechod ('Well of Sin') in Anglesey, and Ffynnon Angau ('Well of Death') in Carmarthenshire were also once cursing wells. Alternatively, they may have served in other nefarious rites, such as the ceremony undertaken at Ffynnon Pasg ('The Easter Well') at

Denbighsire. Here one could 'un-Christianise' themselves by first sipping, and then spitting out, three mouthfuls of the well's water with loathing, which empowered one to make a contract with the Devil and work 'black arts'.

Another well with an unholy reputation is the Frog Well in Acton Burnell, which is sometimes called the Causeway Well on account of its position on the Roman road known as 'the Devil's Causeway'. In Charlotte Sophia Burne's *Shropshire Folklore* (1883), it is described how, 'out of a ferny, flowery bank [this] most beautiful spring rises, which drips into a deep rocky basin, partly natural, of great grey slabs of stone, placed there by the hands of man.' The waters of this spring are 'always cold in summer and warm in winter', and whilst they are credited with a blessed power to heal sore eyes, they also have a sinister side:

> Here the Devil and his imps appear in the form of frogs. Three frogs are always seen together, these are the imps. The largest frog, being Satan himself, remains at the bottom and shows himself but seldom.

The association of the devil and his demons with frogs and toads was once a common article of belief. Illustrative are the beliefs that witches kept toads as familiars, could turn themselves into toads, and fed consecrated Hosts to the Devil, who appeared to them in the form of a toad. The Devil also plays a prominent role in the obtaining of the toad-bone, which bone was believed to confer the power of witchcraft upon its bearer.

Unsurprisingly, curse wells were also favoured by witches and wizards, and at Ffynnon Oer ('the Cold Spring') in Llanddona, the witches who caused the wellspring to issue forth invoked many terrible curses through its waters. Moreover, the waters of Ffynnon Fednant (Caernarvonshire) were used by a wizard to practice his sorceries.[45]

The belief that certain holy wells and springs serve as fountains of natural justice is not confined to Britain. In France, for example, there are numerous such hot-points in the landscape, and many resorted to these wells to commend their enemies' names to the concomitant

45 Jones, *The Holy Wells of Wales*, pp. 118, 129–30.

saints. Illustrative is a spring near Argent (Cher), which was dedicated to Saint Mauvais (Saint Evil). At this spring people could pray to Saint Mauvais for the death of enemies, love rivals, relations standing in the way of inheritance, and similar. Fortuitously for the victims, the spring was situated near the chapel of Saint Bon (Saint Good), where honest folk could seek protection.

Another locus where imprecatory prayers were uttered for preternatural aid was a shrine standing upon a hill rising from the right bank of the river Jaudy, opposite Tréguier (France). The shrine was once an ossuary and was all that remained of a ruined chapel of the Sacrament built around 1600. The chapel was named for Saint Sul (Saint Sulien), but was later re-dedicated to Notre Dame de la Haine (Our Lady of Hatred). In the ossuary were piled numerous saintly statues, including those of Our Lady of Mercy, Our Lady of Good Help, Saint Sul (Sulien), Saint Loup, Saint Antoine, Saint Etienne, Saint Claude, and two statues of Saint Yves, the older of which became known as Saint Yves-de-Vérité (Saint Yves of Truth). Over time the latter statue became the most revered of the ossuary's saintly icons, and became de facto the patron saint of this charnel house-cum-oratory.

During his lifetime Saint Yves was a judge, and after his canonisation was made patron saint of lawyers and judges, for which reason he is prayed to by those seeking justice. Of all his icons, most efficacious were those portraying him in the guise of Saint Yves-de-Vérité (or Saint Ivo ar Virioneg as he is known in Breton), and there were several such statues throughout Brittany, and another in the chapel of St. Yves in Paris (near to the Sorbonne).

Those desiring revenge would go by night to a statue dedicated to St. Yves-de-Vérité, where they would pray for divine justice to be upon their enemy. Individuals commended to the saint were believed to die within a year. As one writer bemoaned in 1620, there are those who 'will abuse pilgrimages, and pray to Saint Yves or some other saints, to avenge their own passions, and to make dead those who have angered them'.[46]

Petitioners typically gave their enemies' names over to St. Yves for the obtainment of justice, rather than out of spite—as was often the

46 François Duine, *Revue des Traditions Populaires*, Volume 27, p. 139.

case with imprecatory petitions made to holy agencies—and some believed maledictions made before his statuary only took effect if the motivation was righteous and the curse deserved. In this case, the Saint was asked to play the role of judge, jury, and executioner. For example, when a pregnant woman was abandoned by her lover in 1901, she gave his name to St. Yves to secure justice. Likewise, when a wealthy landowner and former magistrate issued tough terms driving his tenants to ruin, they dedicated him to the Saint. When a sailor found it difficult to find work after his wife was slandered, the name of the responsible widower was also handed over to the Saint for justice.[47]

In parts of Côtes-d'Armor (France), those who were owed money would say a mass to Saint Yves-de-Vérité, which caused their money to be returned within the year and their debtor to perish.[48] As a Saint of Justice, St. Yves-de-Vérité was also called upon to make judgement regarding serious disputes. For example, if during a disagreement one of the parties invoked St. Yves whilst casting a coin upon the floor (preferably before a statue of the Saint), the one who had lied or was in the wrong would die within the year.[49]

Whilst these magico-religious practices were not authorised or approved by the church, they were popular amongst the poor and dispossessed, who having little recourse to official justice could instead turn to this Saint, who was renowned for aiding the poor and dispensing punitive justice. Indeed, writing in 1830 of the statue at Notre Dame de la Haine, one chronicler reported how in the evening, 'shameful shadows crept furtively towards this sad edifice, placed atop of a hill...they are young pupils weary of their guardian's surveillance, wives abused by their husbands.' The pilgrim would then say three Aves in honour of Notre Dame de la Haine (Our Lady of Hate), and the victim would die within a year.

Other commentators described how a special rite to petition Saint Yves-de-Vérité was required to secure saintly intercession. For this reason supplicants employed the services of 'professional pilgrims', who not only knew the rites and prayers needed to secure the victim's death,

47 Devlin, Judith, *The Superstitious Mind*, p. 20.

48 Paul Sebillot, *Popular Customs of Upper Brittany*, p. 190.

49 Ibid., 190.

but also the whereabouts of those statues having the necessary power. This was risky business, as in 1620 the Catholic Church excommunicated those who, 'in love with revenge', sought out statues of Saint Yves-de-Vérité.

At Tréguier, several local old women proclaimed to be specialists in the kinds of prayers needed, and their ritual formula of offering, adjuration, and condemnation had allegedly been passed from one generation to the next. In return for financial recompense, these impoverished women would intercede on behalf of the interested party, and recite the necessary prayers in front of the oratory in the client's place. These ritual specialists are somewhat comparable to the British guardians presiding over holy wells, stones, and statues, whose role is to watch over and/or administer the associated rites. Illustrative are the guardians overseeing the rites of St. Cuimin at Kilcummin and the guardians of Ffynnon Elian.

The accounts of the rites undertaken by professional pilgrims suggest the procedure for petitioning St. Yves was not entirely set in stone. However, it typically involved circling the murderous statue three times, and repeating specific words and deeds in triplicate. Illustrative is the case of a man who desired his enemy should suffer the same misfortune he had caused others, and so employed the services of an old woman, who agreed to visit the statue at Tréguier on his behalf. She made petition to St. Yves by going about the chapel three times and dipping three scrolls into the holy water.[50] These scrolls are suggestive of St. Yves' role as a judge, and in iconography he is typically represented with a rolled paper in his left hand and a purse in his right, the latter representing his generosity to the poor.

One professional pilgrim, named Anna Bouz, who often journeyed to the Tréguier statue on behalf of others, adjured the murderous Saint by thrice repeating the Penitential Psalm *De Profundis* (*Psalm* 129, 'Out of the depths'), which was said for the souls of those having no-one to pray for them. She then said to the statue, "You know why and for whom I have come; you have been paid; do justice."[51] Pilgrims to the Tréguier statue were also described as 'abjuring him [Saint Yves-de-Vé-

50 Duine, *Revue des Traditions Populaires*, Vol 26, p. 293.

51 Devlin, *The Superstitious Mind*, p. 19.

rité] with certain formulas', and saying to him, "You were just in your life; show that you are still." Those commended to the Saint in this manner were said to die within the year.[52] A more involved operation to secure St Yves' judgement is recorded in Anatole le Braz's *The Legend of Death in Lower Brittany* (1893):

> *To dedicate someone to Saint Yves-de-Vérité, you must:*
>
> 1. Slide a liard [a small French coin] into the shoe of the person whose death is desired.
> 2. Whilst fasting, make three consecutive pilgrimages to the house of the saint; Monday is the dedicated day.
> 3. Take hold of the saint by the shoulder and shake him roughly, saying:
>
>> "You are the little saint of Truth (*Zantik-ar-Wirione*).
>> I *vow* you such.
>> If the right is for him, condemn me.
>> But if the right is for me, let him die within the prescribed time."
>
> 4. At the feet of the saint deposit an offering of eighteen deniers marked with a cross.
> 5. Recite the usual prayers, but begin at the end and say them backwards.
> 6. Circle the chapel three times, without turning the head.[53]

Perturbed by such customs, in 1879 a priest of Tréguier, Father Kerleau, shut the murderous statue away in the sacristy of his church and had the sanctuary destroyed. However, even with the statue removed, people continued to make pilgrimage to the site of the sinister ossuary, where they knelt to seek the Saint's aid in the time-honoured fashion. More daring pilgrims would even knock on the rector's door and ask to see the Saint, but were turned away with varying degrees of politeness.

52 Sebillot, *Popular Customs of Upper Brittany*, p. 190.

53 Le Braz, Anatole, *The Legend of Death in Lower Brittany*, pp. 224–5.

This motivated some to consign the priest himself to the Saint's ruthless judgment, and within a year of removing the statue, and just after finishing Sunday's High Mass, the priest unexpectedly died, which many locals saw as the vengeance of the Saint. As a result, far from ending the custom, the priest's actions ultimately served to reinforce the statue's wonder-working reputation.

Sadly, on 28th May 1928 this infamous and wonder-working wooden statue of Saint Yves-de-Vérité was burned after being discovered at a boarding house of the Augustinian convent (Tréguier). However, another still exists at the nearby chapel of Saint Yves-de-Quintin (Côtes-d'Armor).[54]

In Britain, a far simpler method of invoking maledictions through holy power involved the would-be curser to light a candle in the first church they came to, and there recite the Pater, Ave, Credo, and other prayers backwards over the lit flame.[55] The Lord's Prayer was often recited in reverse for harmful magic, and whilst the use of backward prayers is commonly associated with diabolic magic and the invocation of infernal forces, it also has affinity with other traditional 'Christian' curse practices employing 'backward' deeds to obtain judgment and vengeance upon sinners. Typical of the 'backwards' imprecatory rites used by self-identifying Christians are:

Circling widdershins around a holy well.
Walking a pilgrimage route in reverse.
Turning a 'prayer' stone anti-clockwise upon a bullaun.

Like the clamour made through mortification of things holy—wherein holy icons, religious statuary and the crucifix were covered, turned to the wall, placed upside down, or laid upon the floor—these invertive and sacrilegious acts were intended to goad God, Christ, and his holy retinue into lending numinous aid; the mortified icons were only 'righted' when the wish was granted, which is essentially tantamount to blackmail.

54 For more on this wonder-working statue, see Gwendal Gauthier, *Saint Yves-de-Vérité; the Murderous Statue* (2008) and Anatole Le Braz, *The Legend of Death Among the Armorican Bretons* (1902).

55 Devlin, *The Superstitious Mind*, pp. 18–20.

Another curse worked by inversion of Christian praxis is the 'Reversed Journey', which was elucidated by the Irish scholar, Douglas Hyde:

> This is the way in which the 'Reversed Journey' is carried out. A person is to go to Chapel, and then to make the 'Journey', i.e., the Stations of the Cross, backwards: that is, to begin the 'Journey" at the last picture, XIV, and to finish at the first – all the time invoking the Devil, and asking him to send misfortune and bad luck upon the hated enemy.

Whilst this account refers to an invocation of the Devil, it is questionable whether the pilgrim was really expected to pray to the Devil, or whether this was Hyde's own spin on what he saw as an essentially 'anti-Christian' act. Indeed, Hyde relates how:

> ...only a little while ago an old woman went to a priest, and told him that such and such an injustice had been done to her, and, says she, "I'll go to the church till I make a 'Reversed Journey' for him." The priest explained to her that it was a great sin to make a curse of that kind, but he had great work before he got her to submit and promise that she would not do it.[56]

If the old woman had really intended to pray to the Devil for help, it seems unlikely she would have approached a priest and told him about it. It is more plausible this Christian woman believed the curse to work by grace of God, perhaps in the manner of a clamour, and it was the priest (who saw the practice as devilish) who re-interpreted her prayer to God as a prayer to the Devil.

Such practices demonstrate how laypeople were not averse to using Christian rites in unsanctioned ways for the procurement of preternatural aid. These rites frequently used blessed sacraments and holy sites as a vehicle for harm, including church, shrine, graveyard, and holy well.

56 Hyde, *The Religious Songs of Connacht*, pp. 238–5.

For example, in the early 16th century the Italian jurist Paolo Grillandi wrote how common folk sprinkled holy water over wax images to baptise them. Waters taken from fonts and holy wells were also mixed with earths and clays to make effigies of victims, which could then be put to uses fair and foul.

In the 13th Century the Bishop of Durham ordered that all church fonts should be kept locked down in order to prevent 'the sacred lymph of baptism' from being stolen and used for magical purposes, which included the baptism of poppets for love, lust, fertility, cure, and curse. To circumvent this, some attempted to smuggle their poppets upon baptismal candidates, so the doll was baptised with them. However, in 1554 the Bishop of Roskilde sought to prevent this by declaring children should come to their baptism naked, 'so that people versed in magic shall not be able to hide their dolls with the child to have it baptised and then used for witchcraft.'[57]

The practice of baptising images was thought so prevalent that it appeared in the standard adjuration composed by the 14th Century French inquisitor, Bernard Gui, for the confession of magical practitioners, and is the very first mentioned heresy:

> I, [name], of such and such a place, and such and such a diocese, having been brought before the tribunal, in the presence of you, [name], such and such an inquisitor, do adjure all errors and heresies raising themselves up against the Catholic faith of our Lord Jesus Christ; and in particular I abjure all baptising of images or other non-rational objects...I abjure the art and method of making images from lead or wax or any other material in order to bring about illicit effects...
>
> Bernado Gui
> *Practica Inquisitionis Haereticæ Pravitatis*, 1320

In Ireland, corn dollies were similarly used for imprecatory purposes. Before proceeding the operant visited a church and stood with their

57 Ankarloo and Clark, *Witchcraft and Magic in Europe, The Period of the Witch Trials*, p. 59.

back to the altar whilst making certain prayers. Afterwards they plaited wheat sheaves into an effigy, which was struck in the joints with pins, and buried near the victim's house—in wet soil for a quick death and dry soil for a slow and painful one; here, the speed of the doll's decay directly correlated with the speed of the spell's effect. In the 19th Century a girl was brought before the Ardee police court (County Louth) for making one of these straw dolls. She had been caught walking abroad at night with a pail of water so as to douse the burial site, and thereby speed the effigy's decay.[58]

Not all acts of image magic required anthropomorphic representations, for by power of imagination anything could be made to represent the victim. Indeed, the historical record is replete with examples of objects such as stones, eggs, onions, and toads being used as a proxy for the spell's intended recipient. For example, in the Summer of 1696, a woman was seen furtively clambering over the wall of a churchyard in Söhnstetton (Germany), and there burying three twigs in a child's grave, over which she said, "So as the twigs grow in the ground, so shall brother-in-law perish from the earth, in the name of the Father, the Son, and the Holy Ghost." Soon after the spell was cast, the brother-in-law fell sick. He was not only afflicted with an 'infirmity in the limbs', which left him bed-ridden, but he also stopped eating, which caused him to 'become more like a skeleton than a man'. However, once the three twigs were dug up, the victim returned to health, and his sorcerous sister-in-law was imprisoned for four weeks.[59]

Christian powers were also solicited in the empowerment of an old Malay charm. A waxen poppet the length of a footstep was transfixed from head to toe and wrapped in linen, as one would a corpse, after which prayers were made over it, as though making prayers over the dead. The enshrouded effigy was then buried in the middle of a path regularly frequented by the victim, whilst saying:

> "It is not I who am burying him,
> It is Gabriel who is burying him."[60]

58 Newall, *The Witch Figure*, pp. 81–2.

59 Bever, *Realities of Witchcraft and Popular Magics in Early Modern Europe*, p. 156.

60 Frazer, *The Golden Bough*, pp. 13–4.

This spoken charm is a variation of the 'it is not my hand which does this deed, but [spirit's name]' formula, and through it the hand of the magician becomes 'ridden' or guided by the spiritous entity, in this case the archangel Gabriel, whose name means 'God is my strength'. By carrying out the deed in the name of a spiritous intercessor, the spell becomes empowered through holy agency. It also diminishes the magician's responsibility for the outcome, for in saddling the liability and guilt upon the shoulders of Gabriel, the blood is on the archangel's hands rather than the magicians. Herein the intercessor becomes a 'scapegoat' absolving the operant of any guilt or 'sin'; the angelic agency being better able to bear the burden than a mortal.

An alternative method was to strike the effigy with punitive barbs whilst urging God and his holy retinue to be angry with the victim, and to punish them in a corresponding manner. This approach is driven by the supplicant's belief that their own personal enemy is also the enemy of God, for which reason God should be on their side. An example of this method, wherein symbolic deeds are wedded with imprecatory prayers and psalms, is the following spell from an Arabic Coptic Christian manuscript, which instructs the magician to etch *Psalm* 96 upon a wax image and say:

> O Lord, just as I am angry at this image, may you be angry at [name of victim], son of [name of victim's mother].[61]

Afterwards the wax doll is buried in a tomb that is not visited.[62] Whilst this spell partly relies upon the magical principles of 'image-making' (the effigy) and *similia similibus* (the burial within the tomb), it is clear an element of spirit mediation is also expected, which heavenly aid is secured by the use of Psalm and an appeal to God. Such methods likely originated in ancient Egypt, where pin-struck and tortured graven images were often tied to, or placed with, lead tablets that had been etched with petitions to gods and spirits, and then buried in a tomb or cemetery.

61 Pinch, *Magic in Ancient Egypt*.

62 Mirecki and Meyer, *Magic and Ritual in the Ancient World*, p. 432. Henein and Banquis, *La Magie Par Les Psaumes*.

The manipulation of poppets to 'show the spirit(s) what to do' is also found in witchcraft, with the familiar spirit serving as the agency delivering the curse. Illustrative is the 1579 case of the Windsor Witches, where Mother Dutton was accused of pricking the heart of a waxen doll with a hawthorn spine whilst Mother Devell commanded her familiar, *Bun*, to 'plague him [the victim] and 'spare him not' (*A Rehearsal Both Strange and True*). However, even those accused of witchcraft often employed Christian prayers and scripture in their spells, as illustrated by the case of the French witch, Macette.

In 1391, Macette was tried in Paris, and her charges included the use of a wax effigy to torture her abusive husband, Hennequin de Ruilly. During the trial Macette confessed to invoking Lucifer by thrice calling upon him, and petitioning him to help put Hennequin in such a condition that he would never be able to beat or abuse her again. Whilst making her plea, Macette mixed white wax with pitch, and once these were combined she again called upon Lucifer that he might help, advise, and comfort her. With this done, Macette recited the Gospel of St. John, the *Pater Noster*, and *Ave Maria* three times in succession, conceivably to empower the mixture. She then moulded the pliable medium into the shape of her husband, all the while calling upon Lucifer for help, and again thrice reciting the Gospel of St. John, the *Pater Noster*, and *Ave Maria*. She then boiled a brass vessel filled with water, and cast the graven image into it. Whilst the effigy boiled away she drew three crosses upon its waxen body by point of knife, and several times turned and tormented the poppet in the water using the knife's sharp end and other-times a brass spoon. Through Macette's spell, Hennequin was caused to fall ill and suffer severe stabbing pains.

To increase her husband's torment Macette repaired to some clay pots in which she kept toads for the purposes of vengeful magic, which creatures she fed on white bread and breast milk. Standing before the unopened clay pot she would thrice call upon Lucifer for help, afterwards reciting three times the Gospel of St. John, the *Paternoster*, and *Ave Maria*. She would then open the earthenware pot and stab the toad with long needles or small iron spikes, so her husband would become restless, weak, and sick.

Whilst these dark magics caused Hennequin much agony, a friend persuaded Macette to destroy the graven image, and set free the toads she had pricked to torture her husband. This speedily returned Macette's husband to full health. However, when her deeds were uncovered, Macette was burned at the stake for maleficia.

Particularly noteworthy is Macette's use of the Gospel of St. John, which is a fairly common component of ritual magic. For example, one 17th Century magical manuscript exhorts the magician to boil a bewitched individual's urine in a pan and recite the Gospel of St. John over it. Needles are then dipped into the boiling urine as a charm is said, which serves to return the bewitchment to its sender, and delivers the offending witch to the fiery torments of hell.[63]

The Gospel of St. John is also called for in several magical books, including the *Grimoire of Honorius*, and the *Black Raven*. The latter is attributed to the infamous Renaissance magician, Johann Faustus, and within it the magician is advised:

> Before you summon, it is good to read the Gospel of St. John that begins with the words, "In the beginning was the word...", and you read it up to the words, "...full of grave and truth." Then you go onto the works [i.e., the summoning etc.].

The Gospel of St. John is also recited during the summoning and dismissal of spirits in an anonymous 16th Century book of magic. Such usage suggests St. John's Gospel was believed to have the power to compel spirits to do as the magician commanded, which coercive power is further alluded to in one of the manuscript's conjurations, wherein the magician summons the spirit, "by the dreadful sentence that Saint John gave out against all those spirits that came not but disobeyed..."[64] This Elizabethan manuscript also calls for the magician to recite St. John's Gospel prior to summoning the spirit of Satan into a bowl of water, which waters are then used for the purposes of finding out things past, present, and future. It is also used prior to a conjuration summoning the spirit of Oberon, King of the Fairies.[65] St. John's power to compel spir-

63 Sloane 3706 and Additional MS. 36674, The British Library.

64 Harms, Peterson, and Clark (eds.), *The Book of Oberon*, p. 310.

65 Ibid., 353.

its to heed the magician's call is also evoked in a conjuration for summoning the spirits guarding buried treasure, which are conjured "by the head of Saint John Baptist."[66]

Within this manuscript, the Gospel of St. John is also used at the end of rites of conjuration to give the spirits licence to depart.[67] This conceivably draws upon St. John's ability to expel unwanted spirits by power of baptismal water, which power is also evoked by the purificatory rites magicians undertake prior to magical workings, thereby preserving them from the corrupting influence of any evil spirits conjured.

The commanding and dispersing power of St. John's Gospel is also illustrated by a magical rite to disperse a waterspout, which calls upon the use of a black-handled knife, suggesting a link with Solomonic magic. The rite is described in *Travels into the Levant* (1687) by the French botanist and traveller, Jean de Thévenot:

> ...one of the ship's company kneels down by the mainmast, and holding in one hand a knife with a black handle, he reads the Gospel of St. John, and when he comes to pronounce these holy words: "et verbum caro factum est, et habitavit in nobis," the mariner turns toward the waterspout, and with his knife cuts the air athwart the spout, as if he would cut it, and they say that it is really cut, and lets all the water it holds fall with a great noise.

Since the Middle Ages, St. John's Gospel was also used by lay-people for protection against evil spirits, and was sometimes applied in exorcisms. Indeed, in *The Most Strange and Admirable Discoverie of the Three Witches of Warboys* (1593), it is related how the first chapter of Saint John was read before the possessed victim, Elizabeth Throckmorton, and 'at the hearing whereof she was as one besides her mind; [but] when he that read held his peace she was quiet.'

Considering the prevalent magical use of St. John's Gospel, it is conceivable Macette was aware of its sorcerous application, and her recitations of John's Gospel, along with the *Ave Maria* and *Paternoster*, were

66 Ibid., 321.
67 Ibid., pp. 111, 283.

perhaps intended to compel Lucifer to appear and do her bidding. This would constitute an attempt to adjure and constrain a nefarious power by means of a holy power, which is characteristic of contemporaneous magical practice. Indeed, magical practitioners often drew equally upon heavenly and infernal powers, which they set in opposition or yoked together by power of will for the achievement of their desire.

Illustrative is a spell from the *Grimoirum Verum* to curse an enemy, where nails taken from an old coffin were driven into a victim's footprint with a stone, whilst saying, '*pater noster upto in terra*' ('our father who art on earth'). These are the opening lines of the so-called Witch's Paternoster, which was an inversion of the Lord's Prayer and addressed to 'Our Father, who art on earth' —the land-dwelling Devil as fallen angel. Following this prayer the Devil was petitioned to, "cause harm to N [victim's name], until I remove thee [the nail]." To break this spell, the magician had to pull the nail out whilst saying:

> "I remove thee so that the evil which thou hast caused to N [victim's name] shall cease.
>
> In the name of the Father, and of the Son, and of the Holy Spirit.
> Amen."

Herein the magician makes an appeal to the holy powers to break the unholy curse. The spell laid by the Devil is afterwards lifted through the opposing power of God, which demonstrates the magician's proclivity to traffic with powers both malefic and benefic. This is to reveal the magician as one having dual-allegiance to the light and dark powers, reified in the West as God and the Devil. Wise are those who are both saint and sinner, knowing the proper application of both powers for the realisation of Desire.

In the medieval period, the church was a repository of supernatural power, which could be dispensed to the laity through word and deed in order to aid in daily life, as exemplified by the giving of blessings, healing, and protection. This cultivated a belief that the church, its liturgy, and holy items, were a source of power that could be used in folk rites, which is affirmed by the magical use of church keys, rosaries, consecrated tapers, communion wine, holy waters from the font, earth from churchyards, dusts from altars, and paint and plaster scraped from religious statuary. In addition to religious accoutrements, the church and its grounds were also considered to have magical power, as were the rites said within its walls, which is exemplified by the practice of empowering poppets by placing them beneath the altar.

An example of the vengeful use of holy items is preserved in *Dives and Pauper* (1536), where it is written that dripping wax from a Holy Candle onto a man's footprint whilst saying the Paternoster would cause the victim's feet to rot. Similarly, in 1543, Joanna Meriweather of Canterbury cursed Elizabeth Celsay by dripping wax from a holy candle onto her excrement.[68]

A consecrated Host could also be used to gain revenge on an enemy by naming it for the victim and then stabbing or burning it, much as if it were an effigy. Through this analogical deed the nails of immolation became evocative of the torturous barbs that pinioned Christ to the Cross. Sometimes the Crucifix itself was immolated, with the hope the victim would suffer as Christ did upon the Cross. Illustrative is a transgressive magical practice from Rhineland, where on Good Friday an archer would shoot three or four arrows at an image of the Crucified Christ, believing it would enable him to successfully kill an equal number of enemies every day in battle, which practice is also condemned in the *Malleus Maleficarum*.[69]

This praxis is somewhat evocative of the iconography of St. Sebastian, which Christian soldier was bound to a tree and shot at with arrows. As a desecratory rite, it is also redolent of the *clamour*, with Christ's ire being provoked by the immolation of the Crucifix, which anger is then sublimated towards the victim. Herein, the nails hammered into the effigy with vengeful intent become as physical correlatives of imprecatory prayer and petition, thereby working to arouse the indwelling spirit into action.

The practice of striking nails into the Crucifix is comparable to the treatment of *nkisi* effigies in the Congo Basin. These spirit-filled wooden effigies are petitioned for various reasons, including the bringing

68 Thomas, *Religion and Decline of Magic*, pp. 48–9.

69 Merrifield, *The Archaeology of Ritual and Magic*, pp. 190–1.

of health, wealth, and good fortune, as well as for hunting down and catching thieves, witches, and enemies. Most efficacious for obtaining vengeance is that class of *nkisi* known as *nkondi*, meaning 'the hunter.' These fearsome effigies are typically made with raised hands bearing weapons, and are erected upon a box containing objects giving it power. To gain revenge, the wronged individual licks a nail and violently hammers the spittle-coated barb into the idol whilst shouting, thereby awakening the *nkondi's* spirit. Being angered at the injustice the victim has suffered, the spirit flies forth from the nail-struck effigy and seeks out revenge on their behalf. Herein, each metal thorn embedded in the figure's corpus becomes as a petition delivered unto the idol, awakening or enraging the spirit into action, and cleaving an aperture for the release of its spirituous power.

Before the turn of the 18th Century, the indwelling spirit was awakened and provoked by simply banging or striking the *nkisi*, and some scholars believe the practice of hammering nails or knives into the figure was incepted when the Congolese came into contact with the motif of Christ's Crucifixion. Indeed, many native peoples considered Christ to be the most powerful *nkisi*:

> ...[the crucifix and *nkisi* are both] objects of power that are aroused/resurrected after being nailed, and evidence suggests that many Kongolese understood the crucifix as yet another powerful *nkisi*.[70]

Some scholars speculate the immolated *nkisi* possesses additional correspondence with St. Sebastian, who was bound to a tree with cord and pierced by arrows. St. Sebastian is often depicted with a face enraptured with the pleasure and pain of sexual and spiritual ecstasy, evoking the role of suffering and sacrifice upon the path to attainment. Herein the penetrative arrows and nails become as phalli exciting the corpus, a dual interpretation enciphered in the word *thrill*, meaning 'to pierce, penetrate (as in 'an arrow thrilling through his heart'), and excite'.

Whether or not the Christian motifs brought by the Portuguese missionaries to Central Africa influenced the nailing of *nkisi*, there is

70 Edmonds and Gonzalez, *Caribbean Religious History*, p. 106.

little doubt the image of the Crucified Christ and the tree-bound arrow-struck St. Sebastian became syncretised with the tradition.

Another popular method of preternatural retaliation was to pray the rosary against an enemy, which sometimes involved the invocation of saints. Particularly popular was St. Michael, who is both the warrior of God and defender of the faith. The Christian rosary is especially associated with Mary, and in 1214 Our Lady appeared before St. Dominic, who was struggling to stamp out the Albigensian's heresies, and gave him a rosary, which she said could be used as a spiritual weapon to defeat all enemies of the faith. Later, during the 15th Century, the Dominican priest Alain de la Roche incepted the establishment of the 'fifteen rosary promises (or mysteries)' after a visitation by Our Lord, Our Lady of the Rosary, and St. Dominic. Amongst the promises made by Mary were that, 'what you ask through my Rosary, you shall obtain', and that 'those who propagate my Rosary shall obtain through me aid in all their necessities'. This gave rise to the conception of the rosary as 'need beads', which could be used to pray for outcomes both fair and foul.

The vengeful use of the rosary is demonstrated by events occurring during the 1571 Battle of Lepanto, when the allied Christian forces attempted to prevent the Ottoman Turks from acquiring the Venetian Islands. To aid in this endeavour, the Dominican Pope Pius V encouraged Europe to pray the rosary against the invading fleet, and organised a 40-hour devotion in Rome, which was to take place whilst the battle ensued. Through Marian intercession the vastly outnumbered Christian fleet miraculously defeated the Muslim invaders, and during the battle an apparition of the Blessed Virgin Mary in her aspect of Our Lady of Victory is said to have appeared to the enemy. In memory of this victory won by divine intercession, the day of the battle (7th October) is known as 'the Feast of the Holy Rosary'. The custom of praying the rosary to obliterate an enemy is one that has been employed in numerous battles and disputes ever since.

5

The Imprecatory Psalms

THE 150 POEMS constituting the book of *Psalms* were written over a period encompassing the early monarchy to post-Exilic times, and thus reflect varying stages of Israel's history. Many of the Psalms thus promulgate the idea of there being a special relationship between God and the people of Israel, and, more germane to this discussion, the idea that Israel's enemies are the enemies of God, and vice-versa. A number of Psalms even call upon God to slay these enemies:

> If only you, God, would slay the wicked!
> Away from me, you who are bloodthirsty!
> They speak of you with evil intent;
> your adversaries misuse your name.
> Do I not hate those who hate you, Lord,
> and abhor those who are in rebellion against you?
> I have nothing but hatred for them;
> I count them my enemies.
>
> *Psalm* 139:19–22

Several of the Psalms recount deeds God has undertaken to help deliver the Israelites from their enemies. Illustrative is *Psalm* 136, which details the slaying of the firstborn in Egypt, the overthrowing of Pharaoh and his army, and the defeat of the Canaanite kings. Numerous Psalms also beseech God to remember His covenant with the people of Israel, and to deliver them from their oppressors, which entreaties essentially serve as petitions to God for vengeance against enemies. This vengeful aspect of God is addressed in a direct fashion in *Psalm* 94:1, 'O Lord, you God of vengeance, you God of vengeance, shine forth!'

Many of the Psalms open with a lament or a petition, and end with a thanksgiving. This has led to the speculation that the Psalms were originally liturgical in nature, and that between the recitation of the petition and the thanksgiving the priest or prophet would have given an unwritten and extemporised oracle or blessing assuring the worshipper(s) of a successful outcome.[1] An example of a Psalm that opens with a petition and ends with a thanksgiving, and thereby implies an assumed intervention, is *Psalm* 28:

The petition

To you, O Lord, I call;
you are my rock, do not turn a deaf ear to me.
For if you remain silent,
I will be like those who go down to the pit.

Hear my cry for mercy as I call to you for help,
as I lift up my hands toward your Most Holy
Sanctuary.

Do not drag me away with the wicked,
with those who do evil,
who speak cordially with their neighbours but
harbour malice in their hearts.

Repay them for their deeds and for their evil
work;
repay them for what their hands have done
and bring back on them what they deserve.

Because they have no regard for the deeds of
the Lord and what his hands have done,
he will tear them down and never build them
up again.

The thanksgiving

Praise be to the Lord, for he has heard my cry

1 Barton, *A History of the Bible*, pp. 124–6.

for mercy.
The Lord is my strength and my shield;
my heart trusts in him, and he helps me.
My heart leaps for joy, and with my song I
praise him.
The Lord is the strength of his people,
a fortress of salvation for his anointed one.

The Psalms have been used for magical purposes since the earliest days of Christianity, certainly from at least the 3rd Century, and their construction is thought to have been influenced by the hymns and prayers of ancient Babylonia and Egypt. The magical use of Psalms is found widely in early Christian magic, and of the ninety-three known Christian parchment and papyrus amulets from the 4th–8th Century, at least thirty-one quote from the Psalms.[2]

The manner in which the Psalms are used for magico-religious purposes are many and varied, and span a plethora of expressions from the simple recitation of Psalms to their use in complex ritual procedure. In a magical context, the Psalms are articulated in a number of differing languages, including Hebrew, Latin, Greek and English. This suggests the essential power of the word is retained regardless of the language into which it is translated.

The Psalms have found use in rites of divination, healing, protection, conjuring, exorcism, and cursing. However, most germane to this work are the 'imprecatory Psalms', which were used for casting out demons, witches, and evil spirits, and also for the purposes of invoking punishment upon wrongdoers and enemies. Perhaps the most renowned of these imprecatory Psalms are:

Psalm 5 Give ear to my words, O Jehovah, Consider my meditation. Hearken unto the voice of my cry...The arrogant shall not stand in thy sight; Thou hatest all workers of iniquity. Thou wilt destroy them that speak lies; Jehovah abhorreth the blood-thirsty and deceitful man...Hold them guilty, O God; Let them fall by their own counsels; Thrust them

2 Kruger, *The Gospel of the Saviour*, 2005, p. 29.

out in the multitude of their transgressions; For they have rebelled against Thee.

***Psalm* 35** Strive thou, O Jehovah, with them that strive with me: Fight thou against them that fight against me. Take hold of shield and buckler, And stand up for my help. Draw out also the spear, and stop the way against them that pursue me...Let them be put to shame and brought to dishonour that seek after my soul; Let them be turned back and confounded that devise my hurt. Let them be as chaff before the wind, And the angel of Jehovah driving [them] on. Let their way be dark and slippery, And the angel of Jehovah pursuing them...Let destruction come upon him unawares; And let his net that he hath hid catch himself; With destruction let him fall therein...Stir up thyself, and awake to the justice due unto me, Even unto my cause, my God and my Lord...Let them be put to shame and confounded together that rejoice at my hurt: Let them be clothed with shame and dishonour that magnify themselves against me.

***Psalm* 58** The wicked are estranged from the womb: They go astray as soon as they are born, speaking lies...Break their teeth, O God, in their mouth; Break out the great teeth of the young lions, O Jehovah. Let them melt away as water that runneth apace; When he aimeth his arrows, let them be as though they were cut off. Let them be as a snail which melteth and passeth away, Like the untimely birth of a woman, that hath not seen the sun...The righteous shall rejoice when he seeth the vengeance: He shall wash his feet in the blood of the wicked; So that men shall say, Verily there is a reward for the righteous; Verily there is a God that judgeth in the earth.

***Psalm* 69** Let their table before them become a snare; And when they are in peace, let it become a trap. Let their eyes be darkened, so that they cannot see; And make their loins continually to shake. Pour out thine indignation upon them, And let the fierceness of thine anger overtake them. Let their habitation be desolate; Let none dwell in their tents. For they persecute him whom thou hast smitten; And they tell of the sorrow of those whom thou hast wounded. Add iniquity unto their iniquity; And let them not come into thy righteousness. Let them be blotted out of the book of life, And not be written with the righteous.

***Psalm* 83** O God, keep not thou silence: Hold not thy peace, and be not still, O God. For, lo, thine enemies make a tumult; And they that hate thee have lifted up the head...Do thou unto them as unto Midian, As to Sisera, as to Jabin, at the river Kishon; Who perished at Endor, Who became as dung for the earth. Make their nobles like Oreb and Zeeb; Yea, all their princes like Zebah and Zalmunna; Who said, Let us take to ourselves in possession The habitations of God. O my God, make them like the whirling dust; As stubble before the wind. As the fire that burneth the forest, And as the flame that setteth the mountains on fire, So pursue them with thy tempest, And terrify them with thy storm. Fill their faces with confusion, That they may seek thy name, O Jehovah. Let them be put to shame and dismayed forever; Yea, let them be confounded and perish; That they may know that thou alone, whose name is Jehovah, Art the Most High over all the earth.

***Psalm* 109** Hold not thy peace, O God of my praise; For the mouth of the wicked and the mouth of deceit have they opened against me; They have spoken unto me with a lying tongue. They have compassed me about also with words of hatred, And fought against me without a cause. For my love they are my adversaries; But I give myself unto prayer. And they have rewarded me evil for good, And hatred for my love. Set thou a wicked man over him; And let an adversary stand at his right hand. When he is judged, let him come forth guilty; And let his prayer be turned into sin.

> Let his days be few; And let another take his office. Let his children be fatherless, And his wife a widow. Let his children be vagabonds, and beg; And let them seek [their bread] out of their desolate places. Let the extortioner catch all that he hath; And let strangers make spoil of his labour. Let there be none to extend kindness unto him; Neither let there be any to have pity on his fatherless children. Let his posterity be cut off; In the generation following let their name be blotted out. Let the iniquity of his fathers be remembered with Jehovah; And let not the sin of his mother be blotted out. Let them be before Jehovah continually, That he may cut off the memory of them from the earth; Because he remembered not to show kindness, But persecuted the poor and needy man, And the broken in heart, to slay them. Yea, he loved cursing, and it came unto him; And he delighted not in blessing, and it was far from him. He clothed himself also with cursing as with his garment, And it came into his inward parts like water, And like oil into his bones. Let it be unto him as the raiment wherewith he covereth himself, And for the girdle wherewith he is girded continually. This is the reward of mine adversaries from Jehovah, And of them that speak evil against my soul...Help me, O Jehovah my God; Oh save me according to thy loving kindness; That they may know that this is thy hand; That thou, Jehovah, hast done it...Let mine adversaries be clothed with dishonour, And let them cover themselves with their own shame as with a robe. I will give great thanks unto Jehovah with my mouth; Yea, I will praise him among the multitude. For he will stand at the right hand of the needy, To save him from them that judge his soul.

The language of these imprecatory Psalms resemble petitions for justice, with the supplicant going to great pains to emphasise how the wrongdoer is not only a personal opponent, but also an enemy of God. To this end, the Psalm's author typically details the wrongdoer's many sins and un-Christian behaviours—accusing them of being slanderers, liars, and so forth—and then seeks to cajole God to punish them accordingly.

The simplest method to access the Psalms' power is through oration, and examples of the formal chanting of Psalms for imprecatory purposes abound in Irish hagiographies. For example, during a contest with King Diarmait, St. Ruadhán and his monks fasted and rang their bells against the king whilst singing Psalms of cursing and vengeance. That very night, the sons of the twelve kings of Tara, who were lodging with Diarmait, all met with sudden deaths.[3]

Another example of a saint cursing through *sailm escaine* ('cursing psalms') concerns a confrontation between St. Patrick and a druid named Lochru. When Lochru mocked St. Patrick and his faith, Patrick prayed to God to lift the druid up and remove him from life. In answer to this imprecatory prayer, Lochru was miraculously lifted into the sky and then dropped, falling headfirst onto a rock, which killed him outright. When Lochru's pagan armies assembled to avenge the druid's death, St. Patrick thundered the opening lines of *Psalm* 68, "let God arise and His enemies be scattered and those who hate him be put to flight." Suddenly, a great darkness descended upon the pagan army and in the ensuing confusion they slew many of their own number.

When choosing Psalms for imprecatory purposes, the supplicant typically selects one expressing the nature of the curse they wish to be upon their enemy. For example, in 1117 the annalist recording the murder of Máel Brigte, the son of the head of the church of Kells, evoked the spectre of vengeance by citing *Psalm* 33:17, 'The face of the Lord be against those committing these wickednesses, that He may wipe out their memory from the earth.' Another example is found in an excerpt from an 8th Century Christian text (Berlin MS 8503), which details how *Psalm* 115:4–8 is used as a curse, causing the victim to become as lifeless as the statues of the heathens by power of *similia similibus*:

> ...[he] has hands but he cannot touch; he has feet but he cannot walk; he has eyes but he cannot see; he has ears but he cannot hear; he has a nose but he cannot smell; he has a

3 Bitel, 'Saints and Angry Neighbours; The Politics of Cursing in Irish Hagiography'.

> mouth but he cannot speak a word through his throat; he has a heart but he does not understand.
>
> *Psalm* 115:4–8

Other popular examples include:

To invoke a generational curse

> *Psalm* 20:10—'You will destroy their offspring from the earth. And their children from among the sons of men.'
>
> *Psalm* 137:9—'Happy shall he be, that taketh and dasheth thy little ones against the stones.'

To curse a victim to death

> *Psalm* 54:16—'Let death be upon them. And may they descend alive into hell.'

For loss of home and power

> *Psalm* 68:26—'May their homes be deserted. And may no one live in their tents.'

To stop liars and deceivers

> *Psalm* 58:16—'God, shatter their teeth in their mouths; Lord, tear out the fangs of the young lions!'

Other times the supplicant chooses Psalms expressing the desire in a more symbolic manner, such as *Psalm* 58:8, which reads, 'As a snail which melteth, let every one of them pass away; like the untimely birth of a woman, that they may not see the sun.' This verse seemingly alludes to the idea that the mucous trail left behind a travelling snail is tantamount to the snail dissolving or melting away, or perhaps signifies a belief that an empty snail shell represents a snail that had melted away. Either way, the intent is clear, 'as the snail melts away, so too may the victim waste away and disappear'.

More involved than the formal chanting of Psalms is the practice of combining them with ritual acts and symbolic deeds, such as the recitation of imprecatory Psalms over a wax poppet or lit taper. Several such examples are found in an early 18th Century Arabic Coptic Christian manuscript, although there is evidence that parallel Arabic variants may have existed since the 11th Century:

***Psalm* 48** If you want a person to be sickly, write it [the psalm] on an unfired potsherd and bury it in the fire of a mudbrick hearth and then draw the image of the individual and therefore he will wheeze in good time.

***Psalm* 55** Write [the psalm] on a sheet of copper on Tuesday at the time of Mars and draw on it an image of a woman who you want to haemorrhage, while making it [the image] in wax. You bury it in an irrigation canal running towards the east. Therefore she will haemorrhage.

***Psalm* 78** If it [the psalm] is written with the blood of a Nile catfish from the well of a spring on a white piece of paper, and you wrap a red silk thread around it, and you place it in a pierced new red clay jug, and you put the end of the red thread through the hole, and you seal the mouth of the jug and bury it under a watercourse [running] to the east, and you write at the end of the psalm, 'Run blood of 353 (meaning the name of the woman you want to haemorrhage) just as the waters run on this writing.' Then as a result she haemorrhages and it does not cease until the jug is removed from the canal.

***Psalm* 96** If it [the psalm] is written on a piece of wax in the name of the person whom you want and the name of his mother and you say, "O Lord, just as I am angry at this image, may you be angry at so-and-so, son of so-and-so", and bury it in a tomb that is not visited.

***Psalm* 103** If you have enemies that you fear, then take frogs equal in number to them and tie the frogs' forelegs behind their back with a red silk thread. You read the psalm seven times over each one, and you write the name of the enemy on their backs before you read. After that you put them in a new red earthenware vessel, write these letters [the magical glyphs found in the manuscript] on the pot, seal it with white potter's clay, and bury it in a forgotten tomb. You will see wonders, God willing.[4]

Conforming to ancient magical principles, the majority of the above not only rely upon *similia similibus* for their effect, but also employ a proxy of the victim, whether a potsherd, a drawing of the victim, a wax effigy, or a frog. Notably, in the final exemplar the author also affirms the preternatural effect to be procured by the power and grace of God rather than any demonic entity.

Comparable to the above are the various psalm spells of the Syrian Christian tradition. Illustrative is a curse written in a Syriac Psalter from the Syrian Monastry in Wadi Natrun (Egypt), which handwritten note instructed the would-be curser to put mustard seed and water in a new pot and read *Psalm* 109 over it for three days, and then to pour it on the victim's doorstep, thereby killing him.[5]

The use of Psalms for sorcerous purposes is also found in the Jewish magical tradition, where they are used in the consecration of talismans and the working of spells for protection, health, wealth, and cursing. For example, within the *Cairo Geniza* (a collection of around 300,000 Jewish manuscript fragments) there is an 11th Century Hebrew text that (translated from the Hebrew) reads:

4 Henein & Banquis, *Le Magie Par Les Psaumes: Édition et Traduction d'un Manuscrit Arabe Chrétien d'Égypte*; Mirecki and Meyer (eds), *Magic and Ritual in the Ancient World*, pp. 429–440.

5 Mirecki and Meyer, *Magic and Ritual in the Ancient World*, p. 441.

> To cause someone to haemorrhage. Write on the day of Mars on a blank piece of paper with ink. Bind it in a red silk purse and lay it on a reed. Bury it in a canal running toward the east. This is what you write...

The author then gives the necessary Psalm written in Judeo-Arabic. Some speculate the reason the author gave the instruction in Hebrew, but the Psalm in Arabic, was due to a belief that the Psalm's power might be lost in translation.[6]

The most popular Jewish work on the magical use of Psalms is the *Shimmush Tehillim* ('The Magical Use of Psalms'), which is one of the first texts dealing entirely with the subject, and is thought to date to the 8th Century. This diminutive text is a compilation of the various uses to which Psalms and verses may be put, along with accompanying gestures typical of pan-cultural folk magic, such as burning incense, throwing dust in the direction of one's enemies, and pouring charged water where an opponent lives or frequents. Illustrative is this entry for *Psalm* 109:

> ***Psalm* 109** Have you a mighty enemy, who plagues and oppresses you? Fill a new jug with new sparkling wine, add some mustard to it, and then repeat this psalm for three days successively, while at the same time you keep in mind the holy name of Eel (great and strong God), and afterward pour the mixture before the door of your enemy's dwelling. Be careful, however, that you do not sprinkle a single drop upon yourself when in the act of pouring it out.

Herein *Psalm* 109 is chanted over the vessel to charge the philtre with accursed powers, which are then brought into contact with the victim by pouring the broth where he or she will likely walk, thus transferring the curse to them. The oration of cursing Psalms over powders, liquids, or similar for the purposes of empowering them with imprecatory virtue is found widely in magical traditions, and continues to this very day.

6 Ibid., 441–2.

Other imprecatory uses given in the *Shimmush Tehillim* include *Psalm* 48 to strike terror in one's enemies, *Psalms* 53 to 55 to gain revenge against one's known and unknown enemies, *Psalm* 70 to conquer one's enemies, *Psalm* 94 and 100 to overcome an unyielding and bitter enemy, *Psalms* 110 and 11 to compel one's enemies to bow and beg before them, and *Psalm* 118 to silence heretics, scoffers of religion, and heretics.

The *Shimmush Tehillum* was frequently re-printed in pocket size and translated into several European languages, thereby aiding the dissemination of the practices contained within. Unsurprisingly, it was also placed upon the Catholic Church's *Index of Prohibited Books*.

In addition to Psalms, Jewish magic also used other scriptural passages in the pursuit of satiating desire. A compendium of such practical applications are listed in the 14th Century work, *Sefer Gematriaot*, including several imprecatory uses:

Against an enemy: Ex. 15:5; 15:6; 15:9; 15:19; Deut. 22:6, Is. 10:14 and Prov. 1:17
To cause an enemy to die: Nu. 14–37
To cause an enemy to drown: Ex. 15:70
To cause the strength of an opposing army to wither away: Deut. 4:24
Against pursuers: Ex. 15:4
Against wild beasts: Deut. 18:13
Against a highwayman: Ex. 15:14
Against robbers: Ex. 15:15; Deut. 11:25; Cant. 2: 15; Gen. 32:2–3
Against slander: Ex. 15:7
To cause a man who has sworn falsely to die within a year: Ex. 15:12
To cause a curse to take effect: Lev. 27:29

A survey of the above demonstrates the verses are generally chosen for congruity to intended use. For example, the verse against pursuers (*Exodus* 15:4) comes from Moses' *Song of Deliverance*, and refers to the overcoming of the chariots that pursued the Israelites across Egypt; 'Pharoah's chariots and his host hath he cast into the sea: his chosen captains are also drowned in the Red Sea.' Also, the verse recommended to 'cause a curse to take effect' (*Leviticus* 27:29) runs, 'No person who has been set apart for destruction is to be ransomed, he must be put to death.'

Another book containing instruction for the magical use of Psalms is the 17th Century French text, *Le Livre d'Or* ('The Book of Gold'), which was partly inspired by the *Shimmush Tehillum*. Amongst the charms detailed in this grimoire are several examples of curses to kill or destroy one's enemies, some of which are combined with symbolic ritual actions:

Psalm **7** To vanquish an enemy. Fill an earthenware vessel with water from a spring or river. Over it recite *Psalm* 7:7–17 four times, and then at the end add, 'My God, strike down mine enemies to my feet and trample upon them, as Thou didst bring down the house of Abraham and may they flee from before me.' Then throw this water at a spot where the victim will pass, and you will always defeat them.

Psalm **10 (11)** To curse an enemy to death. Using a bronze pen, write *Psalm* 11:1–7 on a piece of goat parchment, along with certain characters, and place it on the head of a corpse; if the enemy is a man bury it in a woman's grave, and if a woman bury it in a man's grave. The victim will die within a day.

Psalm **36 (37)** Write this Psalm and bury it in front of your enemy's door. His house will be destroyed, his children will die, and all that he possesses will perish.

Psalm **43 (44)** Write this Psalm with bird's blood and bury it in front of your enemy's door and he will be destroyed.

Psalm **61 (62)** Take some powder from under the altar after

Mass has been said and read this Psalm over it seven times. Scatter the dust in front of your enemy's house and if he or she hates you they will be cut down and their house will be destroyed.

***Psalm* 67 (68)** To prevent someone from sleeping, write this Psalm and bury it in front of their door.

***Psalm* 77 (78)** Write this Psalm and certain magical glyphs on the inside of a bronze drinking vessel. Fill it with clean water, say the Psalm over it seven times, and pour the water in front of your enemy's door.

***Psalm* 82 (83)** A number of glyphs are written in a new cooking pot, and the pot is then filled with water in which a woman has washed. The Psalm is said over the water seven times, after which it is poured out in the house of one's enemy and they will be destroyed.

***Psalm* 105 (106)** To sink a ship. Read this Psalm seven times over salt and throw it onto a boat where the sails have spread and it will sink.

***Psalm* 108 (109)** Write out *Psalm* 108:1–20 and wash it with water in which women have bathed on a Saturday. Sprinkle the water in the house of your enemy and the memory of him will be erased from the surface of the earth.

***Psalm* 111 (112)** Take some powdered swallow and read *Psalm* 111:1-8 over it on three consecutive days. Scatter the powder in the house of your enemy and he and all that is of him will perish.

***Psalm* 113 (114 & 115)** Read this Psalm over holy water and spill it over a boat and they will not be able to catch anything in their nets.

***Psalm* 119 (120)** Read this Psalm seven times over water in which a woman has washed herself on a Saturday. Sprinkle it over your enemy's door and he will flee and perish.

Nb. The Psalm numbers given in Le Livre d'Or are based on the Greek (Septuagint) system of numeration, which differs from the Hebrew (Masoteric), and so the Hebrew Psalm numbers have been given alongside in brackets.

Over the centuries the usage of Psalms for the obtainment of desire has passed into many magical traditions, including Hellenic magic, Pennsylvanian German Braucherei (more commonly known as Pow-Wow), the Swedish 'black book' tradition, traditions from the Diaspora of Africa, Voodoo, Hoodoo, Conjure, the Rootworker tradition, the British Cunning Craft traditions, and the Grimoire tradition.

Within the Grimoire tradition the Psalms are sometimes marked upon talismans and pentacles for magical effect. For example, in the *Key of Solomon, Psalm* 109:18 (along with *Deuteronomy* 6:4) is written about the edge of the Fourth Pentacle of Saturn, which serves to execute 'all experiments and operations of ruin, destruction and death.' In addition, the Fifth Pentacle of the Moon, which aids in works of destruction, loss, and the annihilation of enemies, is marked with *Psalm* 68:1, 'Let God arise, and let his enemies be scattered; let them also who hate Him flee before him.'

FOURTH PENTACLE OF SATURN.

FIFTH PENTACLE OF THE MOON.

Psalms were also used for magical purposes by lay-folk, and the use of cursing Psalms was particularly prevalent amongst the poor and oppressed, those for whom recourse to official justice was difficult (if not impossible) to obtain. Such lay practices were more likely inspired by the actions of clergy than books of magic. For example, *Psalm* 109, which was particularly popular in folk curses, was often used by priests for imprecatory purposes, as attested by Reginald Scot in his 16th Century work, *Discoverie of Witchcraft*:

> Certain priests use *Psalm* 108 [109 in Hebrew numeration] as an enchantment or charm, or at the leastwise saying, that against whomsoever they pronounce it, they cannot live one whole year at the utmost.
>
> Book 12, Chapter 17

Many considered *Psalm* 109 to be the most potent and vindictive of the imprecatory Psalms, because it not only asks the Lord to cut short the life of an enemy, but also to place a curse on their family:

> Let their children be fatherless, and his wife a widow. Let his children wander about and beg; and let them seek sustenance far from their ruined homes.

If a dying person said 'the cursing Psalm' (*Psalm* 109) whilst thinking of one who had wronged them, the latter was said to be doomed. Illustrating this belief is a story concerning the cruel and irascible Admiral Sir Cloudesley Shovel (1650–1707), who unjustly condemned a sailor to death. Just as the rope was placed about the sailor's neck, the convicted seaman recited *Psalm* 109. Soon after, the flagship HMS Association and four other ships were wrecked upon the rocks, causing the death of 2000 men. The body of the Admiral washed ashore at Porthellick Cove (St. Mary's, Isles of Scilly), and though he was still alive (albeit barely), a female wrecker cut off his fingers to steal his bejewelled rings, and then buried him alive on the beach. When on her deathbed, the wrecker confessed to her crime, and a stone monument was erected to mark the spot where she had buried him.[7]

The use of 'the cursing Psalm' is also found in Ireland. One example concerns Seán na Raithíneach Ó Murchú (Seán Murphy), an 18th Century poet from Cork, who wrote a lengthy imprecatory poem against a thief who stole a sheep from him. Within the poem Murphy wishes the larcenist's flesh should rot, calls upon devils to torment him, and threatens to unleash 'the cursing Psalm' upon him. Another example concerns the poet Eoghan Rua Ó Súilleabháin, who asked a priest to say the cursing psalm against some soldiers billeted in his home parish, thereby ridding the area of them. The priest suggested the poet should instead compose a mild malediction, which he did:

> Oh Jesus, dear God and Father of the Lamb!
> Who sees us in fetters and in bondage so hard!
> As you made us Christians between Friday and Monday,
> Protect us and banish this scum from us.

This imprecatory poem was repeated by the parishioners over a weekend, causing the troublesome soldiers to leave by the Monday morning.[8]

Psalm 109 was also a popular centrepiece for the German *Totbeten* or *Mordbeten*, although other imprecatory Psalms and mortal curses were also inserted into these 'murderous prayers'.

The praying of the 'cursing Psalm' against enemies continues to this day. Illustrative is a case from 2012, in which a former Navy Chaplin was taken to court in Dallas (USA) for encouraging people to pray *Psalm* 109 against a Jewish agnostic and his Military Religious Freedom Foundation.

In addition to *Psalm* 109, a whole range of imprecatory Psalms were employed by common folk. Illustrative is a Cornish charm to destroy an adder, which involves drawing a circle about the snake, after which the sign of the cross is made over it whilst repeating the first two verses of *Psalm* 68.[9] Another example is the method John Wrightson, the

7 Simon Harris, *Sir Cloudesley Shovell: Stuart Admiral*, 2001.

8 Power, *The Book of Irish Curses*, pp. 68, 87–8.

9 M. A. Courtney, 'Cornish Folklore'. *Folklore*, Volume 5, Issue 1, 1887, p. 207.

19th Century wise man of Stokesley (North Riding, Yorkshire), used to torture and curse those who had overlooked or bewitched an animal. He would pierce an ox heart with nine new pins, nine new needles, and nine new nails and then burn it at midnight whilst reciting two verses from the cursing Psalms. A more involved formula is the 'Eye of Abraham', which combines the use of the seven penitential Psalms with imprecatory prayer and sympathetic magic in order to cause a thief great pain in his eye.

In American Hoodoo, a number of imprecatory Psalms are used in cursing, as demonstrated by the following examples, which were collected by Harry M. Hyatt:

***Psalm* 70** Cut a limb from a tree that is withering, whilst stating which of your enemy's limbs you wish to wither, or elsewise declare your intent to for the victim to wither away entirely. *Psalm* 70 is then read for the victim, and the withered branch is buried with the victim's underwear, which serves to form a link between the spell and the victim.

***Psalm* 119** To control a person, scratch this Psalm onto a brand new tin-pan using a pin or needle, and then hide the pan away so that no-one else can touch it. This spell is somewhat similar to the practice found in *The Book of Gold* of writing Psalms onto a new cooking pot.

The use of Psalms to magically obtain justice and protection is also found in the folk magic of Haiti. For example, when a Haitian immigrant to New York was being sexually harassed in her workplace, a Haitian spirit-worker advised her to:

> Pray *Psalm* 35, let destruction come upon him unawares... and place a snakeskin in your shoe. You will tread soundlessly and slip away from him while he is destroyed by your guardian spirits.[10]

10 Elizabeth McAlister, 'The Benefits of Negative and Aggressive Prayer'.

Conclusion

Whilst curses are often condemned as the work of the Devil, it is clear that many Christians considered maledictions a legitimate answer to the problem of 'sinful' and anti-Christian behaviours. They also saw these curses as being fulfilled by God, and not by demonic entities, and in this were following a convention established by the Bible, which contains countless examples of curses pronounced by God, Jesus, and the Prophets.

When Saints, monks, priests, magicians, and Christian folk sought to place curses, they frequently looked to the Bible for inspiration, often lifting passages from its hallowed pages. Particular favoured were the imprecations of *Deuteronomy* 28 and the cursing Psalms. Other times they drew upon scriptural episodes to create narrative charms, such as those asking God to blight one's enemies with famine and plague, even as He did the Egyptians. To enhance the power of the holy word, whether written or spoken, the chosen passages were sometimes combined with analogical deeds and magical acts, many of which were influenced by folk magic. Whether or not the church agreed with or sanctioned such curses, Christians clearly believed the preternatural effect of their curses to be secured by power of God and his holy retinue rather than the Devil and his demonic horde, which belief served as a potential (if often unsuccessful) defence against accusations of diabolism and witchcraft.

Underpinning the tradition of the holy curse is the principle that God is both creative and destructive, which is attested in *Isaiah* 45:7, 'I form the light, and create darkness; I make peace, and create evil; I the Lord do all these things.' Herein, God's power is revealed to be all-encompassing, and thus capable of deeds both fair and foul. It also presupposes the idea that God and his holy retinue could be cajoled into action through various acts, ranging from simple prayer to ritualistic formulae. Many of these curse rites contain elements inverting practices by which blessings are bestowed, such as walking contra-wise around a holy well, turning a prayer-stone in a widdershins direction, burning a holy candle upside down, and making a backwards pilgrimage about the Stations of the Cross. Herein the one power is shown to have two expressions - a benefic aspect associated with the accepted rites of the church, and a malefic aspect associated with their inversion.

For a self-professed Christian to make a curse in the belief God will answer the call, the individual must consider their motivation to be within the spirit of God's divine word and law. In the Christian cursing tradition, the victim is thus typically made out as being 'ungodly' and un-Christian by rendering them an 'enemy of God', the imprecator is able to justify their invocation of the Lord to smite them down, which strategy is much-favoured by many religions. In a similar fashion, when religious peoples go to war against another, they frequently hold themselves to be the righteous party, and invoke their god(s) against those they deem 'other'.

Naturally, most maledictions are driven by a desire for justice against a perceived wrong. However, even when motivated by personal vengeance and a desire for retribution, Christians have typically clothed these in the guise of 'divine justice' and a desire to demonstrate God's power and keep His law on earth.

When it comes to magic, it is often said there is no black or white magic, there is just power. Certainly, when it comes to the practicalities of magic, a single act of power can be viewed as black or white, good or evil, dependent upon the manner in which it affects the individual or group. Typically, powers and magic benefiting an individual or group are deemed 'good', whilst those working against them are deemed 'evil'. As a result, curses uttered by clerics to bolster the security of the Church and its faithful were generally considered licit and 'good', whilst those curses threatening the security of the Church—including those hurled by non-authorised lay-folk and non-Christians—were considered illicit, evil, and the work of the Devil.

However, whether a curse is the work of priest-craft, witch-craft, or folk-craft, very few individuals (if asked) would believe their imprecation to be un-warranted, and most would be capable of justifying their actions using their own adopted moral or religious code. The Western world only accepts God's punitive miracles as 'righteous' and 'acceptable' because the power originates from their chosen God, and because the motivational factors conform to the moral code of their own chosen religion. Yet, whilst Christians claim their imprecations to be 'divine judgement', they frequently condemn those pronounced by non-Christians and those of other denominations as being the work of the Devil, whether or not the other party accepts the existence of their Devil.

In modern times, curses are still pronounced in the name of God and his holy retinue, both by self-professed Christians, and those who follow a syncretic or pantheistic path that facilitates the inclusion of sainted ones into their belief system. In the time-honoured tradition, they turn to scripture and historical custom for guidance in petitioning the holy powers to bring the forces of evil, or the vengeance of God, upon those they consider their adversaries and the enemies of their Faith.

Bibliography

Ankarloo and Clark, *Witchcraft and Magic in Europe, The Period of the Witch Trials.* University of Pennsylvania Press, 2002.

Barnum, Priscilla Heath. *Dives and Pauper Volume 2*. Oxford University Press, 2004.

Bartlett, Robert. *Why Can the Dead Do Such Great Things?* Princeton University Press, 2015.

Barton, John. *A History of the Bible.* Viking, 2019.

Bever, Edward. *The Realities of Witchcraft and Popular Magic in Early Modern Europe*. Palgrave MacMillan, 2008.

Budge, E. A. Wallis. *Egyptian Magic.* K. Paul, Trench & Trübner, 1901.

Burges, Rev. Dr. C. *No Sacrifice nor Sinne to Aliene or Purchase the Lands of the Bishops*, 1659.

Cannell, Fennella (ed). *The Anthropology of Christianity*. Duke University Press, 2006.

Chumbley, Andrew D. *The Azoëtia* (Sethos Edition). Xoanon, 2002 (1992).

Cullen, Tom A. 'When Black Magic is Afoot, the Aged Rector Simply Has to Curse.' *Desert Sun*, Number 133, 7th January, 1964.

Curtis, Mary. *Antiquities of Laugharne, Pendine, and their Neighbourhoods.* Clay, Sons and Taylor, 1880.

Craine, David. 'Sorcery and Witchcraft in Man in the 17th and 18th Centuries'. *Journal of the Manx Museum* IV, 1939.

Davies, Owen. *Grimoires*. Oxford University Press, 2010.

——— *A People Bewitched; Witchcraft and Magic in Nineteenth Century Somerset*. David & Charles, 2012.

——— *Popular Magic*. Bloomsbury Academic, 2003.

Devlin, Judith. *The Superstitious Mind: French Peasants and the Supernatural in the Nineteenth Century*. Yale University Press, 1987.

Drogin, Marc. *Anathema! Medieval Scribes and the History of Book Curses*. A. Schram, 1983.

Duine, François. *Revue des Traditions Populaires* Volume 26, 1911.

Edmonds and Gonzalez. *Caribbean Religious History*. NYU Press, 2010.

Foxe, Edward. *Actes and Monuments*. John Day, 1563.

Frazer, George James. *The Golden Bough*. Macmillan & Co., 1894.

— *Folk-Lore in the Old Testament: Studies in Comparative Religion, Legend, & Law*. Macmillan & Co., 1919.

Groome, Francis Hindes. *In Gipsy Tents*. William P. Nimmo & Co., 1880.

Harbison, Peter. *Pilgrimage in Ireland: The Monuments and the People*. Syracuse University Press, 1992.

Harms, Clark & Peterson, *The Book of Oberon*. Llewellyn, 2015.

Harris, Simon. *Sir Cloudesley Shovell: Stuart Admiral*. Spellmount Limited, 1999.

Henein & Banquis, *Le Magie Par Les Psaumes: Édition et Traduction d'un Manuscrit Arabe Chrétien d'Égypte*, 1975.

Hole, Christina. *Witchcraft in England*. Collier/Macmillan, 1945.

Howard, Michael. *West Country Witches*. Three Hands Press, 2010.

——— *East Anglian Witches and Wizards*. Three Hands Press, 2017.

Hyde, Douglas. *The Religious Songs of Connacht: A collection of poems, stories, prayers, satires, ranns, charms, etc.* M.H. McGill & Son, 1906.

Ihnat, Kati and Katelyn Mesler. 'From Christian Devotion to Jewish Sorcery: The Curious History of Wax Figurines in Medieval Europe'. In *Entangled Histories:* Knowledge, Authority, and Jewish Culture in the Thirteenth Century. University of Pennsylvania Press, 2017.

Johnson, Thomas K. *Tidebast och Vandelröt: Magical Representations in the Swedish Black Art Book Tradition.* ProQuest Dissertations, 2010.

Jones, Francis. *The Holy Wells of Wales.* University of Wales Press, 1954.

Kieckhefer, Richard. *Forbidden Rites.* University of Pennsylvania Press, 1998.

Kent, Benedict H.M. "Curses in Acts; Hearing the Apostles' Words of Judgement Alongside 'Magical' Spell Texts" *Journal For the Study of the New Testament*, Volume 39 Issue 4, 2017.

Kruger, Michael J. *The Gospel of the Saviour.* Brill Academic Publishers, 2005.

Le Braz, Anatole. *The Legend of Death in Lower Brittany.* 1893.

Lingard, John. *History of the Antiquities of the Anglo-Saxon Church.* Edward Walker, 1806.

Little, Lester K. *Benedictine Maledictions.* Cornell University Press, 1993.

——— *Monks & Nuns, Saints & Outcasts; Religion in Medieval Society.* Cornell University Press, 2000.

——— 'The Separation of Religious Curses from Blessings in the Latin West'. *Memoirs of the American Academy in Rome,* Vol. 51/2, 2007/7.

Mathers, S.L. Macgregor. *The Key of Solomon the King.* Weiser Books, 2000 (1889).

Maxwell-Stuart. *The British Witch.* Amberley Publishing, 2014.

McAlister, Elizabeth. 'The Benefits of Negative and Aggressive Prayer'. *The Immanent Frame,* 2014.

Merrifield, Ralph. *The Archaeology of Ritual and Magic.* New Amsterdam Books, NY, 1987.

Mirecki, Paul and Marvin Meyer (eds). *Magic and Ritual in the Ancient World.* Brill Academic Publishers, 2001.

Moore. *The Folklore of the Isle of Man.* 1891.

Murray, Margaret. *The God of the Witches.* Faber & Faber, 1931.

Newall. *The Witch Figure.* Routledge & Kegan Paul, 1973.

Notes and Queries for Somerset and Dorset, 1885.

Pennant, Thomas. *Tours in Wales, Vol. 3.* Wilkie and Robinson, 1810.

Pinch, Geraldine Harris. *Magic in Ancient Egypt.* British Museum Press, 2006.

Power, Patrick C. *The Book of Irish Curses.* Templegate, 1974.
Plummer, Charles. *Lives of Irish Saints.* Clarendon Press, 1922.
Rustad, Mary, ed. *The Black Books of Elverum.* Galde Press, Inc., 2006.
Skinner, J. 'A Ten Days Tour Through the Isle of Anglesey, December 1802.' *Archaelogia Cambrensis Supplement,* July, 1908.
Stokes, William. *The Life and Labours in Art and Archaeology of George Petrie.* Longmans, Green and Company, 1868.
Thomas, Keith. *Religion and the Decline of Magic.* Scribner, 1971.
Trevelyan, Marie. *Folklore and Folk Stories of Wales.* E. Stock, 1909.
Young, Francis. 'The Dissolution of the Monasteries and the Democratisation of Magic in Post-Reformation England'. *Religions,* Vol 10 Issue 4, 2019.
Waite, A.E. *The Book of Black Magic and of Pacts,* 1898.
Waters, Thomas. *Cursed Britain.* Yale University Press, 2019.
Watson, Lyall. *The Nature of Things; The Secret Life of Inanimate Objects.* Destiny Books, 1996.

Index

This first edition of *Anathema Maranatha* was published by Three Hands Press in October 2022. It is comprised of 5,000 paperbound copies, 1,000 hand-numbered standard hardcover copies bound in black cloth with color dust wraps, and a special edition of thirty-three copies in full black goatskin with marbled endpapers and slipcase, hand-bound by Andy Rottner.

Scribæ Quo Mysterium Famulatur